P.S.

ALSO BY STUDS TERKEL

American Dreams
Lost and Found

Chicago

Coming of Age
The Story of Our Century by Those Who've Lived It

Division Street
America

Giants of Jazz

"The Good War"
An Oral History of World War II

The Great Divide
Second Thoughts on the American Dream

Hard Times
An Oral History of the Great Depression

Hope Dies Last
Keeping the Faith in Troubled Times

My American Century

Race
*How Blacks and Whites Think and Feel
About the American Obsession*

Studs Terkel Interviews
Film and Theater

Talking to Myself
A Memoir of My Times

Touch and Go
A Memoir

Will the Circle Be Unbroken?
Reflections on Death, Rebirth, and Hunger for a Faith

Working
*People Talk About What They Do All Day and
How They Feel About What They Do*

P.S.

Further Thoughts from a
Lifetime of Listening

Studs Terkel

THE NEW PRESS

NEW YORK
LONDON

Published in the United States by The New Press, New York, 2008
Distributed by W. W. Norton & Company, Inc., New York

LIBRARY OF CONGRESS CATALOGING-IN-PUBLICATION DATA

Terkel, Studs, 1912–
P.S. : further thoughts from a lifetime of listening / Studs Terkel.
p. cm.
Includes pieces that appeared in the WFMT magazine, Chicago.
ISBN 978-1-59558-423-6 (pb)
1. Terkel, Studs, 1912—Miscellanea. 2. Broadcasters—United
States—Biography—Miscellanea. 3. Authors, American—20th
century—Biography—Miscellanea. 4. Interviews—United States.
5. United States—Social life and customs—20th century—Miscellanea.
6. United States—Social conditions—20th century—Miscellanea.
7. United States—Intellectual life—20th century—Miscellanea.
8. United States—Politics and government—20th century—
Miscellanea. 9. Chicago (Ill.)—History—20th century—
Miscellanea. I. Chicago (1975). II. Title.
AC8.T38 2008
791.440973'0904—dc22 2008026539

The New Press was established in 1990 as a not-for-profit alternative to
the large, commercial publishing houses currently dominating the book
publishing industry. The New Press operates in the public interest rather
than for private gain, and is committed to publishing, in innovative ways,
works of educational, cultural, and community value that are often
deemed insufficiently profitable.

www.thenewpress.com

Composition by dix!

Printed in the U.S.A.

4   6   8   10   9   7   5   3

For Sydney Lewis

CONTENTS

CONTENTS

Part III

PREFACE
Among My Souvenirs

"AMONG MY SOUVENIRS" was a popular sentimental ditty of the mid-20s. It was to song as Joyce Kilmer's "Trees" was to poetry. Nonetheless, it served my purpose in seeking out this old junk, scattered around and about in what could whimsically be described as my workroom. I was reminded of a gimpy old guy wheeling, with some effort, his huge plastic bag, all of his worldly goods, toward his home under the bridge. A few yards away was a paper-thin old doll, pushing her worldly goods toward home under the bridge. Her frame was skeletal, yet her grip was as firm as a pro-football linebacker's.

So it was with me on my findings in my workroom, which I hadn't visited in years. There were scattered, torn sheets of wrinkled paper under the desk, behind the bookcases, beneath the couch, tossed in boxes, everywhere. I put together two major conversations. One, with James Baldwin, took place shortly after his return from exile in Europe. His new book was a series of essays, titled *Nobody Knows My Name*. This is one of the strongest interviews I've ever done. The other was an old conversation I thought I had lost with E. Y. "Yip"

Harburg. He was perhaps one of the most perceptive as well as committed lyric writers extant.

There were also two documentaries that I had done with Jim Unrath, the resourceful WFMT radio announcer who volunteered to be my engineer. The one documentary, *Born to Live,* was the 1962 Prix-Italia award winner. It was submitted during the Cuban missile crisis, which, for those who may remember, was one of the nation's most traumatic moments. The Prix-Italia was an annual award for radio and TV. It is as prestigious in those worlds as is a Nobel Prize for the written word. The other documentary consisted of voices of the Great Depression. From the fifteen hours of tape collected for use in my book *Hard Times: An Oral History of the Great Depression,* I condensed the words into one tape: *A Gathering of Survivors.* (The situation then was not too removed from the one we face today in the matter of joblessness and need. Today, we use euphemisms: instead of depression, we say recession. But to the man and woman designated out of work, one is a synonym for the other.)

The rest of the book consists of pieces that appeared in the WFMT magazine *Chicago* that have never been republished and that I thought were still interesting.

Here we go.

Part I

SCARING THE DAYLIGHTS OUT OF MA PERKINS, 1974:
Confessions of Butch, Bugs, the Chicago Kid . . . but Not Clark Gable

IN 1934, I became a gangster.

It had nothing whatsoever to do with Bugs Moran or Al Capone or Hymie Weiss or Murray the Camel or the Genna Brothers or Jake Guzik or that most ill-starred of horticultural-ists, Dion O'Bannion. (How often after his sudden passing did I go by Scofield's Flower Shop, so near and dear to Holy Name, and reflect on God's will and *qué será, será*. For it was in that bower, amid roses and orchids and lilies of the valley, that dap-per Dion, with a seasonal flower as his boutonniere, met his maker. He was the minstrel boy who to the war did often go; in this instance, it came to him, as a message from Al.)

True, I did have a glancing acquaintance with the garage where the St. Valentine's Day Massacre occurred. (I glanced in one day, looking for Upsadaisy Conners. He was a sometime mechanic—and at times a soldier for the Mob—who owed my mother six months' rent, coming to about two hundred dollars. He had disappeared. Some weeks later, he was found floating down the drainage canal. A slight misadventure. My mother wore sackcloth and ashes. At least two hundred dollars' worth. Happily, all was not lost. I inherited his silk dressing gown. It was similar to the one worn by Clark Gable as Ace Wilfong in *A Free Soul.* Fortunately, Upsadaisy was my size, not Gable's. Unfortunately, Norma Shearer was not around. As I looked into the mirror, a study in subdued scarlet with thin black stripes, I missed Norma. Though she may have been slightly cockeyed and, as Lillian Hellman observed, had a lovely face unclouded by thought, I missed her terribly. Oh, well.)

No, my gangsterism had nothing to do with the precipitous demise of Dutch Gentleman (What a lovely name for a hood!), his brother, and several comrades-in-arms. Jack McGurn was reputed to have machine-gunned their passage to Valhalla on that celebratory afternoon when boys and girls passed innocently erotic cards to one another. Fortunately for Jack, he had a blond alibi, Louise Rolfe. (In my silk dressing gown, I saw the vision of Louise. I missed her terribly, too.) Unfortunately for Jack, he was remembered on a subsequent St. Valentine's Day and was himself dispatched by a cupid's dart in the form of lead. It was at a fine bowling alley. As he let the three-fingered ball go, he appeared to have made a strike. Jack fell down and broke his crown, but the ninepin did not come tumbling after. It was a bloody spare. Thus was the martyred Christian saint twice memorialized. It was truly a love that passeth understanding.

No, my experience as a paid killer, safecracker, and extortionist was, alas, ersatz. I was a soap opera villain.

My life of crime began in *Ma Perkins*. Ma, a widow, owned a lumberyard. She and her lifelong friend, Shuffles (Was there a twilight something going on between them? We never really knew), her son, John, her daughter, Fay, and her son-in-law, Willie, did the best they could. They endured small-town scandals, back-door gossip, serious illness, and trials Job had never envisioned. Yet, Ma and her tribe of decent Americans persevered. For years and years and years and years, Monday through Friday.

I had nothing to do with any of this. Mine was the incursion of outside malevolence. I, and smooth-talking colleagues from the Big City, would, on occasion, slip into Ma's domain. Not on little cat feet. Ours was a heavy tread.

My first such appearance, indeed my debut as a gangster, was in the person of Butch Malone. He was as brutish a knave as ever terrified a Terre Haute housewife, especially the one who washed her things in Oxydol, courtesy of Procter & Gamble. For six weeks, off and on, I gave Ma and her family an awful time. As Butch, I wound up, if I remember right, in Sing Sing. A life sentence. What was even worse, I was written out of the script.

It was a catch-as-catch-can existence. I'd reappear as someone named Pete or Steve or Bugs or the Chicago Kid. At times, my well-deserved end came in more bloody fashion. I was run off a cliff by some local constable; I was shot by a companion; in all instances, I was disappeared. (In despair, I once asked a director if I couldn't play the good guy for a change, the hero, perhaps. Ruefully, he explained: Heroes had pear-shaped tones; mine were apricot shaped.)

Though Ma Perkins was my most frequent pigeon, I found myself unbearable to Mary Marlin, whose five-day-a-week martyrdom transcended St. Theresa's. (On occasion, my menacing gravel came a slight pause after the last chord of "Claire de Lune" was pressed by Helen Westbrook at the Hammond.)

I was unspeakable to Kitty Keene and obscene to Helen Trent (Can a woman find love after thirty-five?). And I wasn't very nice to "Girl Alone." I was even bad to a girl who was bad to "Girl Alone," in the person of Mercedes McCambridge. Let's face it. I was the most miserable of wretches. I was so vile that in *Betty and Bob*, I once threatened her mother. Or was she *his* mother? The lovely, gracious dowager was played by Edie Davis, who eventually became Ronald Reagan's mother-in-law. Oh, well. (It *is* hard to tell, isn't it, where soap opera leaves off and life begins?)

The dialogue in all these adventures was like none other ever invented. It was truly sui generis. It wasn't Melville. It wasn't Faulkner. Nor could Chekhov ever dream it up. It was, in short, astounding. Most often, it was offered sotto voce. My confederate and I nuzzled up to the microphone in the manner of Bing Crosby and Russ Columbo. But what we crooned boded no good for the good folk.

Boss: You know what to do?
Me: Yeah, boss.
Boss: Synchronize our watches.
Me: Watches?
Boss: Yeah, stupid. Watches.
Me: I gotcha, boss.
Boss: What've ya got?
Me: Eleven.
Boss: Ya got New York time, stupid. It's ten o'clock.
Me: I gotcha.
Boss: Let's go.
Me: Okay, boss.

There was never in the history of drama, whether it be Euripides, Shakespeare, Ibsen, or O'Neill, a pause that was as pregnant as a soap opera pause. Especially when the distraught heroine murmured her troubles to the straight-arrow hero. He was forever WASP. He was Bruce or Charles or James. Sometimes he was Gordon. He was never Angelo or Eli or Wladek. He was certainly never Booker. He was usually a banker. Or a broker. Or a man of considerable property. He was as honest as the day was long. And, God, *were* they long days! The cross he bore was invariably a ne'er-do-well younger brother. She, Cynthia, had a wild younger sister. Talk about troubles. Small wonder they spoke so deliberately, so softly, and oh, so, so slowly. It was this air of monumental patience that enabled them to carry that weight, to gallantly see it through.

Awaiting my cure, I died each day. Each second flew by as quickly as a minute; each minute was as quicksilvery as an hour. Would I were a Zen Buddhist! I had read somewhere that when life is burdensome, take to the Bible. So I reflected on Ruth amid the alien corn. I called on Ecclesiastes, as well: And this, too, shall pass. Thus, in these theological musings, I, too, was enabled to carry that weight, to gallantly see it through. Each of us, in his or her own way, was brave, off mike as well as on. It was chin up all the way. In time, we came to believe the stuff actually was Flaubert and Brontë and Henry James.

Oh, those lovely pauses! What with three solid minutes for commercials, a musical signature, the announcer's introduction, integrating a summary of yesterday's tortuousness—and the pauses—it came to no more than eight minutes of script. And don't forget the soundman. A door opens. Thirty seconds.

There was such care taken: every word, every syllable, the manner in which the heroine said, "Oh?" or the hero said, "Oh?"

I never said, "Oh?" I always said, "Oh, yeah?" Nothing was left to chance. Humanity's fate hung in the balance. Naturally, the performers were not inclined to an ad hoc approach. An ad-lib was sacrilege. Improvisation was *lèse majesté*. But life being real and earnest, as Ma, Mary, Kitty, *Girl Alone*, and Betty and Bob could well attest, an untoward event would occasionally occur.

Was it '39 that a terrible snowstorm hit our city? The cast of *Ma Perkins* was waiting for the scripts. The messenger, it appears, was lost somewhere in the drifts of Wacker Drive. No scripts. Time to go on the air. Let's improvise, suggested the director. Ma and her son, John, are plodding through a snowstorm. The wind is howling. Says John, at one point in time, "Ma, walk behind me. I'll break wind for you." Glory be! It is a memory that blesses and burns.

As for the directors, they were a singular lot. The mark of the master was mastery of the stopwatch. If we got off on time, to the precise second—and the words were spoken and the pauses taken—all else was of small consequence. Anxiously peering into the control room, we saw thumb meet index finger. There were smiles all around. All was well. Another triumphal day. We were Olivier, Edwin Booth, Eleonora Duse. Troupers, all. Artists, all.

One such *regis* (for it was a ballet of words) I shall never forget. He had the appearance of Albert Einstein. I have since met Bertrand Russell, J. Bronowski, Buckminster Fuller, and Erich Fromm, but none of them compared to this one in intellectual bearing. He always sat, chin in hand, in the manner of Rodin's *Thinker*. He was the most impressive-looking man I had ever encountered.

During one audition, he advised, after considerable thought: "Give me Humphrey Bogart." I had just seen Bogey as Duke Mantee in *The Petrified Forest*. I let a cigarette dangle from my lower lip and muttered, hardly opening my mouth, "Get in dere, you guys." He shook his head: "Give me Humphrey Bogart as he was ten years ago." I said, precisely as before, "Get in dere, you guys." He smiled, nodded. "That's it. You got it."

On another occasion, Einstein's look-alike said, "Give me Jimmy Cagney." I jabbed my elbow forward sharply and said, trying out my tenor, "Get in dere, you guys." He was content. At still another time, he suggested, "Give me Eddie Robinson." (Eddie! Well, well. He once said to another performer, "Give me Jack Barrymore.") I was confused: "You mean Edward G. Robinson?" He replied, somewhat snappishly, "Give me him." I pulled out a dime cigar and commanded in my finest nasal, "Get in dere, you guys." He smiled. I was in.

There were times when dialects were called for. Foreign. Especially bad guys. I had an all-purpose dialect, known as Continental. It was guaranteed to baffle, indeed destroy, Henry Higgins. It more often than not was acceptable because it sounded so un-American. Once I slipped into something that sounded Swedish to him. I was supposed to be a middle-European assassin. He stalked impatiently the length of the studio. "That's Swedish. I want something foreign." I was stuck.

"How about Mediterranean?" I tentatively suggested. "They're loaded with assassins." He paused; he studied me. "Hmm. Give it to me." I did my usual Continental. He beamed. "Marvelous. You got it." It *was* marvelous: a three-week job. And I never got to assassinate anybody. Somebody got me. Even now, I remember my last words, as I faded away from the mike, collapsing on the studio floor: "Fugivva me, Mudder of Ooaaawwow!" Thus I died.

"I want Levantine." It was another director. Could it have been *Captain Midnight* or *Little Orphan Annie*? I think it was Daddy Warbucks who was having trouble with a smuggling ring somewhere in the Middle East. Or *was* it Captain Midnight? (Oh, Jim Ameche's pear-shaped tones! They were more pear-shaped than his brother, Don's.) I stared dumbly toward the control room. "Levantine?" He pressed his finger testily, it seemed to me, on the talk-back button. "Yes, of course. Something from the Levant." The only such one I had heard of was Oscar. I did my Continental. He nodded. That, I'm delighted to say, was a four-week job.

My most formidable challenge came during the several auditions of a projected nighttime half-hour drama, *Martin of the Mist*. It was based (Heaven help us all!) on the theme of *The Flying Dutchman*. Horlicks malted milk was interested in sponsoring it at one time. Later, General Mills appeared excited. And, still later, a cigarette company wanted to run it up the flagpole. There were, I believe, four different auditions. Each time, we had a new skipper, a new Martin. John Hodiak was the first. He went to Hollywood. MacDonald Carey was the second. He went to Hollywood. I forget who the third and fourth were. They, too, went west. But, in all instances, I was the Polynesian bo'sun. Einstein's look-alike directed all the versions. For some reason, he felt I was the perfect Polynesian.

The opening lines were mine. "Ma-a-arr-te-e-e-ennn of de Me-e-e-est!" It was repeated about five times. "*Sing* it," Einstein said. "Be mellifluous. Remember, you're from the islands! A child of nature! *Sing* it!" I sang it, thinking all the while of Cio-Cio-San in *Madame Butterfly*. It helped. "Now run around the studio as you sing it." I looked dumbly toward the control room. It was NBC's hugest studio, the size of a small racetrack. It was here that Joseph Gallicchio and the whole symphony orchestra played. In fact, they supplied the musical background. "Run around the *whole* studio?" I mumbled, thinking of Jesse Owens and Paavo Nurmi. *They* never sang while they ran. "Don't you understand?" Einstein was testy again. "You're calling out from a distance. A mist. This is a ghost ship." Oh, I got it.

I ran around the studio, singing out "Ma-a-arr-te-e-e-ennn of de Me-e-e-est." Five times. By the time I reached the mike, I was Phidippides at the end of the marathon. I carried no torch, but I didn't collapse. I was breathing rather laboriously, I must admit. The musicians honored me with a *tusch*. Even now, my heart leaps as I hear the violin bows tapping the music stands.

But Einstein had another leap of the imagination. "Take your shoes off." I looked dumbly toward the control room. "Don't you understand?" He was testy again. "You're Polynesian. They don't wear shoes." Oh, I got it. "May I keep my socks on?" There was a touch of desperation to my voice. I wasn't sure I had showered that morning; I was worried about athlete's foot; and I was certainly athletic at that moment. I waited. So did the whole symphony orchestra. Came the order: "Bare feet. Polynesians don't wear socks. We want to hear the slap-slap-slap of your feet on the deck." To this day, I am confused. How could the slap-slap-slap of my feet be heard a hundred yards away from the microphone? Slowly, I took off my socks. It was okay; I had taken a shower that morning.

It's better with your shoes off. I was saying that to myself, thinking of the Stanislavsky technique. A touch of realism couldn't hurt. It's better with your shoes off. I thought of Beatrice Lillie, too, as she sang "I'm a geisha girl." Her refrain was: "It's better with your shoes off." Thus reflecting, it helped. Once more, I sang out as I ran, a child of nature. When again I reached the mike, I was expecting a standing ovation from the orchestra. Nothing. A fine thing. They stand up for Solti, for Gilels, for Horowitz, for Piatigorsky. Was my performance any less virtuoso? Oh, well.

Polynesians. Levantines. Mediterraneans. Smugglers, assassins, children of nature. Glory moments. But none of these experiences matches the perverse delight of playing the *American* gangster. Even now, as in a mist, I hear my voice, "Get in dere, you guys." I am Bogey, Cagney, Little Caesar. But it's small consolation. I am not Clark Gable. Though that silk dressing gown has long since been taken away by the sanitation man, I think of Norma Shearer. And how I missed her something terrible. Oh, well. I did scare the daylights out of Ma Perkins.

DREAMLAND, 1977

IT IS NIGHTTIME. I am standing outside Dreamland. I am waiting for my brother. It is a ballroom on the West Side of Chicago. Here, black jazz bands play: Lottie Hightower and her men, one night; Charlie Cooke and his friends, another. I am impatiently shuffling my feet, though I do like the sounds I hear wafting through the open windows.

It is not to be confused with the Dreamland Cafe. That's on the city's South Side. Joe Oliver, up from New Orleans, played there a few years ago. He has since moved to Lincoln Gardens, where Johnny Dodds, his brother Baby, and a feisty little woman of a piano player, Lil Hardin, have joined him. His young disciple, Louis Armstrong, has been outblowing Joe and has just been called out East by Fletcher Henderson. A girl who picked up my brother took him to this place a few months ago. He said it was really something.

Here at the ballroom young white men and young women come to dance rather than to listen. Preferably on a dime. To sock. In short, to rub bellies together and, thus, excite one another. Always, toward the end of the night, comes the slow blues for which everybody is waiting.

My daddy looks at the clock
And the clock strikes out
Oh daddy, takes it out
Before it gets too late.

It is a place where young people who work all week as shoe
dogs, secretaries, shipping clerks, and telephone operators—
even nurses—come to dance, make dates, and, they hope,
make love. My brother, a popular shoe dog at the Boston
Store, usually does very well here. He is a natural-born
dancer, tells funny stories, and has a way with the girls. He is
seventeen.

It is 1924. I remember the year quite well. Fighting Bob La
Follette ran for president. There were two other candidates,
one of whom won. It made no difference which. It might have
made a considerable difference had Bob won. That's why he
didn't have a ghost of a chance. He did poll five million votes,
and that was something—he being neither a Republican nor a
Democrat. Nineteen twenty-four. And where have all the
flowers gone?

Oh, I shocked and grievously disappointed Miss Henrietta
Boone. She was my seventh-grade teacher at McLaren. I was
her favorite. I sat in the front row, not merely because I was
short. "Louis," she purred (not Louis as in the Sun King;
she pronounced it as in Lewis Stone, the Prisoner of Zenda),
"are you for Calvin Coolidge or John W. Davis?" Innocently—
or was I damnably perverse even then?—I piped, "Fightin'
Bob La Follette." She was startled, poor dear. Her wig
went slightly askew. I could see the terrible hurt in her eyes.
Why have I upset such gentle hearts? Why couldn't I have
been my cute little button self and said the right thing: "Keep

Cool with Coolidge"? It didn't take much to make her day. I failed her.

*   *   *

In the autumn of 1960, at the reunion of the University of Chicago Law School, class of '34, a straw vote was taken. Kennedy versus Nixon. The luncheon at the Loop Club wasn't bad. The drinks were OK. A nice fat feeling of self-satisfaction all around. Those attending were lawyers who, from appearances, had done not too badly. Slight paunches and jowls closely shaven. The vote was something like: Nixon, 45; Kennedy, 41; Fighting Bob La Follette, 1. A few uncertain laughs. That was all. Several of my fellow alumni looked toward me. They smiled benignly. He's a card, that one. I smiled, too. Charlie Chaplin.

I realize Bob has been dead many years. And yet it is a vote I was too young to cast in 1924. I did tell one luncheon companion, of raised eyebrows, that Bob La Follette, dead, had more blood to him than the two young make-out artists, who were more machine than human. His eyebrows shot up even higher. He turned to another to discuss real estate. I went for another drink. The bar was closed. Oh, the Midway, the Midway, where burning Veblen loved and sang . . .

Miss Boone did forgive me. On inaugural morning, the following March, she allowed me to listen on the school's crystal set as President Coolidge took the oath of office on the front porch of his Vermont home. It was difficult to make out what he said. Perhaps it was because I had only one earphone; the other was being used by Dorothy, another favorite of Miss Boone. Perhaps he had nothing to say.

I could easily make out what Burton K. Wheeler said. During the previous fall, the Montana senator, Fighting Bob's running mate, spoke at Ashland Auditorium. It was only two blocks from my mother's rooming house. (Two years later, she sold it and leased a men's hotel near the Loop.) And one block from Dreamland. My father arose from his sickbed and took me there. He liked Bob La Follette. My mother sniffed. She liked only sure winners. Wheeler was damning the malefactors of great wealth, loud and raspy and clear.

The vigor of his voice forty-five years later astonished me. I had visited his Washington law office in 1969. I was interested in his memories of the Great Depression. The rasp was still there, and the bite. He told of a trembling little senator from Missouri who considered resigning because "they've indicted the old man. He made me everything I am." Tom Pendergast, political boss of Kansas City, was Harry's boss, too. Wheeler had talked Truman out of it. I hadn't the heart to ask whether he thought, in retrospect, he had done the right thing. Harry grew in the presidency, it is said. The impertinent question is hardly asked: Didn't we, in a generation, diminish to his size? At eighty, Wheeler was booming out indignation. As I listened, transfixed, I was back at Ashland Auditorium. And only one block away from Dreamland.

*   *   *

In 1912, the year I was born, the *Titanic* sank. I have never, until now, attached any significance to it. Why is it that one of man's most astounding achievements, the ship that will not sink, did in fact do just that while arrogantly ramming an iceberg? And why is it that I, who have made it a point never to drive a car, depend so much on technology, that is, the arrogant Uher (tape recorder). Will I, one day, encounter my own iceberg?

I am twelve years old. The dance is over. My brother will soon be coming out. I am hanging around for two reasons. My brother, if alone, might treat me to a chocolate malted at Liggett's, and slip me one of those song sheets they pass out at Dreamland: "Yearning," "I Wonder Who's Kissing Her Now," "Louise," "All Alone." I delight as he sings them to me in his light baritone, while I'm sipping a malted through a straw. On Friday evening, he'll take me to the Palace, where the headliners, Van and Schenck, the Pennant Winning Team of Songland, will do wonders with these tunes. Nobody in the world can sing "All Alone" the way Joe Schenck does, in his high tenor, as he sits on the apron close to the audience.

As for the other reason: I am much taken with the music I hear. I had never heard such exciting sounds before. So this is jazz. I am hooked, now and forever.

I see him. He is not alone. There goes my chocolate malted. Oh, well. She's a very pretty girl. Flashy. The others he'd come out with were pretty, too, each in her own fashion, but mousy. This one is quite mature, about twenty. He's probably told her he's twenty-one. He does that often, with girls he takes to one of the vacant rooms of Dixieland. (My mother's rooming house had no such name, but I've since read *Look Homeward, Angel.*) My brother's name is Ben.

I make it a point never to crab his act. He is, in fact, pleased to see me. We have an understanding. He calls on me to see that the coast is clear, that our mother is asleep, that the key to the vacant room is still on the hallway ring and not around her waist.

On several such occasions, after he and his companion have been at it, and she, suddenly guilt possessed, is anxious to get home at once, he gently raps on my door. He's taking her home; she lives to hell and gone; you know the crazy schedule of streetcars at this hour; the bed is badly rumpled. If, in the meantime, our mother were to awaken before his return and make the rounds, as she often does, there would be hell to pay. Will I be a good kid and do the usual? I shut the pages of *The Three Musketeers* at the moment Planchet is spitting into the Seine.

The usual: hurried bare feet to the linen closet; clean sheets, clean pillowcases, a clean Turkish towel; and I'm on my way to Canaan Land. On reaching Canaan Land, it's off with the old and on with the new. The vacant room is now free from signs of sin and ready for a paying guest, God-fearing or not.

A thought occurs to me. Had my luck been better, I might have become a first-rate pimp. Or a candidate for public office. Or even an adviser to presidents.

Ben and his friend reach the curb. Uh-oh. There are three guys on the corner. They approach. The girl appears alarmed and touches Ben's arm. One calls out to her. She doesn't move. Neither does Ben. The guy is really angry. He calls out again. She walks toward him, uncertainly, as though her high heels are giving her trouble. He slaps her hard. Her hand goes to her cheek. She whimpers. He grabs her by the arm and pulls her away. Ben moves toward them. The other two block his way. Each takes him by the arm. Ben resists as they force him toward an automobile parked nearby. Another guy sits at the wheel. I am against the wall, watching. Ben calls out to me.

I know the guy who slapped the girl. His name is Barney. He has been bragging a great deal about how tough he is. And how when it comes to women, he's Rudolph Valentino. How he buys them Pink Ladies and pousse-cafés at the Blind Pig and then takes them to bed. Ben laughs at him. I know why. I have seen my brother, arm in arm, with any number of Barney's girls, on his way to Dixieland. I have seen Barney, turning around and around, bewildered and furious. And alone. On these occasions, as I lean against the wall, I always cross my fingers. I'm afraid Barney may do something desperate.

Barney says he's a member of the 42s; and Ben is gonna get it. Ben finds this brag and threat amusing. He tells me Barney is just a loudmouthed fake. Ben laughs; the 42s aren't that desperate; they haven't scraped the bottom of the barrel yet.

The 42s are junior members of the Syndicate. It's a farm club. What the Toledo Mud Hens are to the New York Giants. They graduate, if they prove their worth, into the big league. I have no actuarial table at hand, but I've a hunch 42 alumni seldom reach the biblical age of three score and ten. Ben may not have been scared a moment ago, but he is now. So am I.

* * *

Two of my classmates at McLaren, Jimmy One and Jimmy Two, talk of one day achieving recognition in this society. They dream of the 42s as North Shore matrons dream of the social register. An older brother of one and a young uncle of the other, 42 alumni, are in the employ of Al Capone, one of our city's most highly regarded citizens. The uncle, a few years later, was seen floating down the drainage canal. And no water wings. It was a strange place for him to have gone swimming. The waters were polluted even then.

My companions chatter incessantly. They confide in me all their Horatio Alger dreams: hard and fanciful work, with its concomitant, the rise to the top, Virtue rewarded.

I have no idea why they have chosen me as their confidant. Why not the parish priest? Perhaps it is because, during examinations, I shove my paper slightly to my right as I move in my seat slightly to my left. Jimmy One, who is seated behind me, moves slightly to his right and leans forward, brow furrowed. He is properly attentive as he glances downward. When his paper is completed, he shoves it slightly to his right, as he moves in his seat slightly to his left. Seated behind him is Jimmy Two.

Miss Henrietta Boone is delighted, though somewhat surprised, that Jimmy One and Jimmy Two do so well on these occasions. They pay so little attention during the rest of the semester. She prophesies: "In my crystal ball, I see three boys who will be successful young Americans, of whom we'll all be proud." She is Jeane Dixon.

How have her predictions come out? Jimmy One and Jimmy Two graduate from McLaren and the 42s into the greater society of the Syndicate. Jimmy One, according to *Billboard*'s latest communiqué, is doing well in the jukebox industry. Occasionally, he makes the financial page of the metropolitan daily. He is the grandfather of seven, and the father-in-law of a young physicist.

Jimmy Two was doing magnificently in the field of fire and bomb insurance. His clients were, in the main, restaurants and taverns. One day, he met with an unfortunate accident. No one quite knows what happened. What is known is that Jimmy Two was found lying in some Chicago alley. The newspaper photograph, slightly fuzzy, shows him quite comfortable: He is staring up at the sky, though it is doubtful whether he sees much of its blue.

And I, the third of Miss Boone's favorite boys, am doing what I've done most of my life: listening to what people tell me.

Aside from moments of perversity, which I find difficult to explain, I am agreeable to most people most of the time. I find in the silent-film comedian Raymond Griffith my alter ego. As a jewel thief, he fled to Mexico with his accomplice. When she felt the need to return to the United States and become respectable, he solicitously drove her back. When his two fiancées insisted on marrying him, he agreed and drove to Salt Lake City. Of course. When people talk to me of their lives, I offer the sympathetic ear. I nod understandingly as I watch the reel of tape revolving. It's tougher with a cassette; there is nothing to watch.

There was a good deal to watch during the Kefauver investigation of organized crime. It was televised. One afternoon, especially, caught my attention. And my heart. Lou Farrell, an Omaha businessman, his hair a distinguished silver-gray, was on the stand. Senator Tobey, the righteous New Englander, was trying to give the witness a hard time. I paraphrase from memory:

"Your name is Luigi Fratto, is it not?" Not Louis, not Lou, nor, for that matter, Lewis. Luigi. What Cromwell was to the Irish, this bald Cotton Mather was to Mr. Fratto's people. A sense of decorum was maintained by the witness. "Senator, you seen too many movies. My name is Lou Farrell." It was offered with the rough grace and that proper note of impertinence of a Cassius Clay telling off inquisitors: "My name is Muhammad Ali." The witness had indeed been Louis Fratto, my McKinley High School fellow alumnus. Was I perverse as, seated before the TV set, I glowed with pride?

Pride cometh before the Fall. I was to make this discovery one balmy spring night. It was a reunion of McKinley graduates. In middle age, we gathered: politicians, lawyers, a doctor, a judge or two, a funeral director, a disc jockey. It was a West Side restaurant built in a rococo style. A huge fountain in the lobby below, with water flowing from out of the generous hands of a sculpted Roman goddess. Angels in stone, smiling beatifically at all the patrons from walls and ceiling. And here, amid all this salubriousness, I experienced mortification.

As a tribute was paid to teachers of the past, to honored alumni, among them Walt Disney, I was called upon. It wasn't too long after Mr. Farrell's television appearance. There was a good round of applause. I spoke of those more traditional schools, far less colorful, that boast of bankers, generals, senators, film stars, and philanthropists among their alumni. They are as nothing, I proclaimed. We of McKinley High have produced stars of the highest-rated show in the history of TV—the Kefauver Quiz. Where I had expected appreciative laughter, there was a dead silence.

The toastmaster, a judge well respected by Mayor Daley, whispered hoarsely, "For shame, Studs, for shame." From the tables, I saw only smoke rings from Upmann Fancy Tales, being thoughtfully puffed. Oh God how I tried to recover, to win back the affection of my fellows. I talked of old glories, of our baseball teams that lost 15 to 2, of basketball teams that lost 95 to 23. I told fast and funny stories of the olden days: of Old Powles, a nineteenth-century remainder, of Mr. Brimblecom, of scraggly gray beard and mean, nasty, nasal putdowns of "Mediterraneans," and of Mr. Potter, who favored his prize students with subscriptions to the *Dearborn Independent*, Henry Fords's anti-Semitic journal. My words tumbled out, one on top of the other.

I heard one person laugh. It was more of a nervous giggle. As I sat down, two guests clapped their hands in a slow, measured beat. About three claps. At the table, a companion murmured softly, "Kid, you went over like a lead balloon." And yet, in retrospect, it was no ethnic slur at all. I was right in expressing pride.

Consider this. Who have been more patriotic, more devoted to the service of our country in a pinch than those most often condemned by the righteous? Whom did the CIA call upon when, it was felt, our national security was endangered? When harsh measures were demanded, such as the doing in of Fidel Castro, it wasn't your Boston Brahmin or Texas cowboy whose services were requested. It was Momo Giancana, one of the jewels in our city's crown. That he failed was no fault of his disciplined upbringing. And whom did Mayor Daley most often call upon for political support on our city's West Side? Aldermen and ward committeemen, of all ethnic groups, who are faithful mourners of the funerals of some of my more distinguished fellow alumni. And who can ever forget the moving plea of Al Capone, dying in Alcatraz: "Set me free and I'll help you fight the Bolsheviks"? Ask not what your country can do for you, but what you can do for your country.

A profound sense of loyalty extends to friends as well as to country. When one is in trouble, whether with officialdom (something quite easily resolved; cash in hand, preferably brand-new bills, turneth away such wrath) or with matters of the heart (being cuckolded), he can depend on a small circle of friends.

So is it with Barney, outside Dreamland, on this night in 1924. As Ben calls out, "Kid!" I move toward him uncertainly. The back door of the automobile is open. The two strangers appear to be urging him in. "Hiya, Ben," I say, for want of anything better. "How ya doin'?" The others see me for the first time. I have a natural tendency to blend into any background.

"Who're you?" the big one says, slightly puzzled.

"I'm his brother."

"Beat it."

"He's s'posed to be buyin' me a malted."

"He ain't buyin' ya nothin'."

"It's Friday night," I say, apropos of nothing. I'm trembling.

"Yeah," says Ben. His voice is shaking. "A chocolate malted at Liggett's. It's the best in town, fellas."

The driver leans back against the seat. He sighs. "Are we goin' or not?"

"Let's take him too," says the short one.

"Are you nuts?" counters the big one.

"Aw, Christ," moans the chauffeur. "Make up your mind."

"Where's Barney?"

"He's gone off with his pig."

They look at one another. What's to be done? Should I suggest we all go for a malted? Always, I've been in favor of peaceful solutions.

"My mother is sick," I blurt out.

"Too bad," says the big one.

"She's callin' for Ben. That's why I came to get him."

The big one turns to my brother. "Is that your name?" Ben nods quickly. About five times.

"OK, *Ben*. Get the fuck out of here. If we ever catch you foolin' around with our women, you're gonna wind up in the drainage canal. All wrapped in cement. Y'unnerstan'?"

Ben understands.

"Yer lucky you got a little brother."

Ben nods.

"An' yer lucky yer mother's sick."

Ben nods.

The big one reaches toward his inside pocket, smiles, and says, "Run!" Ben and I take off. We hear laughter as we run and run and run, without once looking back.

Exhausted, we lean against a fence gate. Ben touches my cheek. He pats me on the head. We walk. I reach for his hand.

It is cold and sweaty. Mine is too. It is the final scene from *The Bicycle Thief*. He is the humiliated father and I am the small boy, Bruno Ricci.

*   *   *

Rome, 1962. Vittorio De Sica is seated in his office. His classic face betrays weariness. I observe we're within hailing distance of the balcony from which Il Duce addressed multitudes. He smiles. He quotes Baudelaire on Napoleon: A dictator is not as dangerous alive as when he lives on after death.

"You had your sorry period," he says. "McCarthyism. We had a bad one after the war." Closet Fascists gave him a hard time. They were in high circles of government.

Once a matinee idol, he still acts in films, too many of which are bad ones. Reason: He must raise much of his own money to finance the ones he directs. It is better now, but in the beginning the government was intransigent. They abhorred his chosen themes.

Shoe Shine: homeless boys, rootless, roaming streets. *The Bicycle Thief*: unemployment. *The Roof*: housing. *Umberto D*: indigent old age. *Miracle in Milan*: a fable of the poor.

"I've lost all my money on these films. They are not commercial. But I'm glad to lose it this way. To have for a souvenir of my life pictures like *Umberto D* and *The Bicycle Thief*."

The Bicycle Thief is one of my all-time favorites, I tell him. It has affected my life in ways I cannot quite explain. He tells how he chose a simple workingman, a non-actor, as the father. How he began filming without having cast the boy. He had auditioned scores. He was looking for a kid with "human" eyes and a strange, funny little face. As the shooting begins, a crowd gathers. "I see a boy near me. A miracle. 'Why are you here?' I say to him. 'I'm watchin',' he says. 'What is your name?' 'Enzo

Staiola.' How old are you?' 'Five.' 'Would you like to make a picture with me?' 'Yes.' 'Enter. Go.' " De Sica laughs.

"Bruno Ricci," I mumble. "That kid was marvelous."

De Sica looks at me. His face softens. "You remember the name?"

"Sure."

"I am so grateful. It is very emotional to me that an American can remember the name of a little boy like Bruno."

"Mr. De Sica," I say, "I saw the movie twelve times, for God's sake." And for mine, too.

As a farewell token, he offers a poem by the Neapolitan Salvatore di Giacomo. He shuts his eyes and recites. It is a letter to a lost youth and lost love. I don't understand a word. Why then do I weep?

*   *   *

Ben and I stumble toward Dixieland. The vacant room is not occupied that night; nor for many nights to follow. At least, not by Ben.

JAMES BALDWIN, 1961

[OPENS WITH PIANO and Bessie Smith singing]

When it rained five days and the sky turned dark as night,
Then trouble's taking place in the low lands at night.

I woke up this morning, can't even get out of my door.
There's enough trouble to make a poor girl wonder where
    she wanna go.

Then they rowed a little boat about five miles 'cross the
    pond.
Then they rowed a little boat about five miles 'cross the
    pond.
I packed all my clothes so the men, they rolled me along.

When it thunders and lightning and the wind begins to
    blow.
When it thunders and lightning and the wind begins to
    blow.
There's thousands of people ain't got no place to go.

27

Then I went and stood up on some high old lonesome hill.
Then I went and stood up on some high old lonesome hill.
Then looked down on the house where I used to live.

Backwater blues done caused me to pack my things and go.
Backwater blues done caused me to pack my things and go.
'Cause my house fell down and I can't live there no more.

Mmmm . . . I can't move no more.
Mmmm . . . I can't move no more.
There ain't no place for a poor old girl to go.

Of course, Miss Bessie's song is a familiar one today, in the year 2008. Though it was written in 1927, and brought here in 1961 by Baldwin, it's telling us about the recent catastrophe Katrina. We know what happened to the lowlands, Gentilly, and the Lower Ninth Ward in August of 2005. It's an old story with a new refrain.

Bessie sang of it years ago, and Baldwin remembered it in the Swiss Alps, to which he had exiled himself for several years. Bessie Smith, of course, the empress of the blues, singing of a disaster, of a flood.

*   *   *

Sitting with me, hearing Bessie Smith on this recording, is James Baldwin, one of the rare men in the world who seems to know who he is today. As you listen to this record of Bessie Smith, what's your feeling?

It's very hard to describe that feeling. Um . . . [He sighs.] It's a—

The first time I ever heard this record was in Europe, under very different circumstances than I'd ever listened to Bessie in New York. And what struck me was the fact that she was singing, as you say, about a disaster that had almost killed her.

And she'd accepted it and was going—beyond it. It's a fantastic kind of understatement in it. It's the way I want to write, you know. When she says, "My house fell down and I can't live there no more." It's a great—sentence; it's a great—achievement.

The way you want to write, you say. I'm looking now at page five of your new book, and it's a remarkable one: Nobody Knows My Name. *It's a series of essays, articles, opinions of James Baldwin.* More Notes of a Native Son, *the subtitle.*

And on page five—the reason I've chosen the Bessie Smith record—because on page five you write of your being in Europe; you were in Switzerland.

Yes.

And you said you came armed with two Bessie Smith records and a typewriter: "And I began to try to re-create the life that I had first known as a child and from which I'd spent so many years in flight. And it was Bessie Smith who, through her tone and her cadence, helped me dig back to the way I myself must have spoke when I was little. And I remember the things I had heard and seen and felt; I buried them deep." "I had never"—and here's the part—"I had never listened to Bessie Smith in America (in the same way that, for years, I never touched watermelon). But in Europe, I reconciled myself."

Yes, well, how can I put that? That winter in Switzerland, I was working on my first novel, which I thought I would never be able to finish. And I finally realized, in Europe, that one of the reasons that I couldn't finish this novel was that I was ashamed of where I'd come from and where I'd been. And ashamed of life in the church, and ashamed of my father, and ashamed of the blues, and ashamed of jazz, and of course ashamed of wa-termelon. Because it was, you know, all of these stereotypes that the country afflicts on Negroes: that we all eat water-melon; that we all do nothing but sing the blues and all that.

Well, I was afraid of all that and I ran from it. And when I say I was trying to dig back to the way I myself must have spo-ken when I was little, I realized that I had acquired so many af-fectations, I had told myself so many lies, that I really had buried myself beneath a whole fantastic image of myself which wasn't mine, but white people's image of me. And I re-alized that I had not always talked—obviously I hadn't always talked the way I had forced myself to learn how to talk. And I had to find out what I had been like in the beginning. And in order, just technically then, to re-create Negro speech, I real-ized it was a cadence, it was a beat much more than . . . It was not a question of dropping *S*s or *N*s or *G*s, but a question of the beat, really. And Bessie had the beat, you know.

And in this icy wilderness, as far removed from Harlem as anything you can imagine, with Bessie Smith and me, I began—

And white snow.

And white snow, and white mountains, and white faces who re-ally thought I was—I had been sent by the devil. It was a very strange . . . They had never seen a Negro before. And in this kind of isolation—it's very hard to describe—I managed to finish the book. And I played Bessie every day. And really, literally—this may sound strange—a lot of the book is in dia-logue, and I corrected things according to . . . what I was able to hear when Bessie . . . sang and when James P. Johnson played. It's that tone and that sound, you know, jazz, which is in me.

The point you made a moment ago—the point you were speaking of—the sense of shame. Did you sense this? The sense of shame of a heritage that is so rich, in accepting the white man's stereotype of yourself.

I'm afraid it's one of the great dilemmas, one of the great psychological hazards of being an American Negro. And in fact it's much more than that. I've seen a great many people go under, and everyone, every Negro in America, is in some way, one way or another, menaced by it.

One's born in a white country, in a white, Protestant, Puritan country, where one was once a slave; where all the standards and all the images that you open your—When you open your eyes in the world, everything you see—none of it applies to you. You go to white movies, you know, and like everybody else you fall in love with Joan Crawford, and you root for the good guys who are killing off the Indians. And it comes as a great psychological collision when you begin to realize all of these things are really metaphors for your oppression and will lead into a kind of psychological warfare in which you may perish.

I was born in a church, for example, and my father was a very religious and righteous man. But, of course we were in Harlem. We lived in a terrible house, and downstairs from us there were, you know, all these, what my father called "good-time" people. There was a prostitute and all of her paramours and all that jazz. I remember I loved this woman. She was very nice to us. But we weren't really allowed to go to her house, and if we went there we were beaten for it. And when I was older, that whole odor of gin, you know, homemade gin, really, and pig's feet and chitterlings and poverty, and the basement.

All of this got terribly mixed up together in mind with the

whole holy roller–white God business, and I really began to go a little out of my mind, because I obviously wasn't white, and it wasn't even a question so much of wanting to *be* white, but I didn't quite know anymore what being black meant. I couldn't accept what I'd been told. And all you're ever told in this country about being black is that it's a terrible, terrible thing to be.

Now, in order to survive this you have to really dig down into yourself and re-create yourself, really, according to no image which yet exists in America, you know. You have to impose, in fact—this may sound very strange—you have to decide who you are and force the world to deal with you and not this *idea* of you.

You have to decide who you are, whether you are black or white. Who you are.

Who you are. And that pressure, the question of being black or white, is robbed of its power. I mean you can still, of course, be beaten up on the South Side by . . . anybody. The social menace does not lessen. But in some way it is a world now which perhaps can destroy you physically, but the danger of your destroying yourself has not vanished, but is minimized.

*The name of the book, if we may—this is directly connected—*Nobody Knows My Name. *For years, you, when I think of you, are known as James. Never known as James Baldwin. Home James, sometimes called George—In the old days Sam—*

Boy.

Or sometimes boy.

Sometimes. [Small laugh]

Nobody Knows My Name. *Why did you choose that title?*

Well, at the risk of sounding pontifical, it's at once . . . I suppose it's a fairly bitter title, but it's also meant as a kind of warning to my country. In the days when people—well, in the days when people called me boy, those days haven't passed, except that I didn't answer then, and I don't answer now.

To be a Negro in this country is really just . . . never to be looked at. And what white people see when they look at you is not really you . . .

Invisible—

You're invisible. What they do see in you when they look at you is what they have invested you with. And what they have invested you with is all the agony, and the pain, and the danger, and the passion, and the torment, you know, sin, death, and hell, of which everyone in this country is terrified. You represent a level of experience which Americans deny. And I think—this may sound mystical—but I think it is very easily proven, you know.

It's proven in great relief in the South when you consider the extraordinary price, the absolutely prohibitive price, the South has paid to keep the Negro in his place. And they have not succeeded in doing that, but have succeeded in having what is almost certainly a most bewildered and demoralized white population in the Western World. And on another level you can see in the life of the country, not only in the South, what a terrible price the country has paid for this effort to keep a distance between themselves and black people.

It was . . . In the same way, for example, it is very difficult, it is hazardous, psychologically—personally hazardous—for a Negro in this country really to hate white people, because he is too involved with them, not only socially, but historically. And no matter who says what, in fact, Negroes and whites in this country are related to each other. You know, half the black families of the South are related to the judges and the lawyers and the white families of the South. They are cousins, and kissing cousins at that, at least kissing cousins. Now, this is a terrible, terrible depth of involvement.

It's easy for an African to hate the invader and drive him out of Africa. But it is very difficult for an American Negro to do this—obviously cannot do this with white people; there's no place to drive them. This is a country which belongs equally to us both. And one's got to learn to live together here or else there won't be any country.

This matter of living together, or this ambivalent attitude that the South has toward the Negro, and the ambivalence perhaps is most eloquently expressed, tragically expressed in the life, the sayings of William Faulkner, the brilliant American novelist who writes a remarkable story, "Dry September," in which he seems to analyze the malaise. At the same time, he himself makes comments that are shocking. You have a chapter in your book dealing with Faulkner and desegregation. And is it this ambivalence too, that—

It's this love, hatred, love, hatred. I hate to think of what the spiritual state of the South would be if all the Negroes moved out of it. The white people there don't want them—you know, want to keep them, want them in their place—but would be terrified if they left. I really think the bottom of their world would have fallen out.

In the case of Faulkner in "Dry September" and *Light in*

August, or even in *The Sound and the Fury,* he can really get, you know, as you put it, to the bone. He can get at the truth of what the black-white relationship is in the South, and what a dark force it is in the southern personality. But at the same time, Faulkner as a citizen, as a man, as a citizen of Mississippi, is committed to what Mississippians take to be their past. And it's one thing for Faulkner to deal with the Negro in his imagination where he can control him, and quite another one for him to deal with him in life, where he can't control him. And in life, obviously, the uncontrollable Negro is simply—is determined to overthrow everything in which Faulkner imagined himself to believe.

It's one thing to demand justice in literature and another thing to face the price that one's got to pay for it in life. And I think another thing about southerners—and I think it's also true of the nation—is that now no matter how they deny it or what kind of rationalizations they cover it up with, they know the crimes they've committed against black people, and they're terrified of these crimes being committed against them.

The element of guilt, then, is here, too.

Yes.

There's a point you make, and very beautifully, somewhere in the book Nobody Knows My Name. *I forget which one of the essays is involved. In the South, the white man is continuously bringing up the matter of the Negro; in the North, never. So obsessed in one case, and so ignored in the other.*

It's very funny. It's very funny especially because the results turn out to be, in the case of the Negro's lot in the world, so very much the same.

But it seems to me it must be absolute torment to be a southerner if you imagine that these people—that one day, you know, one day even Faulkner himself was born, and certainly, when he was born, he was raised by a black woman, probably the model of Dilsey. And one fine day, the child of three or four or five who has been involved with black people on the most intense level and at the most important time in anybody's life—it suddenly breaks on him like a thundercloud that it's all taboo. And, of course, since we know that nobody ever recovers, really, from his earliest impressions, the torment that goes on in a southerner who is absolutely forbidden to excavate his beginnings, you know, it seems to me is a key to those terrifying mobs. It isn't hatred that drives those people in the streets; it's pure terror.

And perhaps a bit of schizophrenia here, too.

Well, by this time it's absolutely schizophrenic. And obviously not only in the South, but the South is a very useful example on a personal and social level of what is occurring really in the country. And the sexual paranoia, you know.

Again it is very important to remember what it means to be born in a Protestant, Puritan country with all the taboos which are placed on the flesh, and to have, at the same time, in this country, such a vivid example of a decent imagination, of paganism and the sexual liberty with which white people invest Negroes, you know, and penalize them for.

The very nature of the American heritage. You seem to be just digging into it right now, the combination of Puritanism and paganism both, and the conflict—

Yes, yes, and the terrible tension—

And the tensions that come as a result.

It's a guilt about the flesh, and in this country the Negro pays for that guilt that white people have about the flesh.

Since you bring up this point—the Negro pays for the guilt that white people have about the flesh—we think, too, about the position of the Negro woman and the Negro man—

My God.

And in this article—you wrote a beautiful article for Tone *magazine— you were saying something about the mistress of the house, the white mistress who admires her maid very much. But she speaks of the no-account husband.*

No-account husband.

So this brings to mind the matter of what it means to be a Negro male.

It connects with that old, old phrase that Negroes are the last to be hired and the first to be fired. And this does not apply to the Negro maid, particularly, though it can. But it absolutely applies without exception and with great rigor to Negro men.

And one's got to consider, especially when one begins to talk about this whole theory, the whole tension between violent and nonviolent. The dilemma and the rage and the anguish of a Negro man, who in the first place is forced to accept all kinds of humiliations in his working day; whose power in the world is so slight that he cannot really protect his home, his wife, his children, you know; and then who finds himself out of work, and watches his children growing up menaced in exactly the same way that he has been menaced. When a child is fourteen—when a Negro child is fourteen—he knows the score already. There's nothing you can do. . . . And all you can do about it is try—is pray, really, that this will not destroy him.

But the tension this creates within the best of men is absolutely unimaginable—and something this country refuses to imagine—and very, very dangerous. And again, it complicates the sexuality of the country and of the Negro in a hideous way exactly because all Negroes are raised in a kind of matriarchy, since, after all, the wife can go out and wash the white lady's clothes, and steal little things from the kitchen, you know, and this is the way we've all grown up.

Now, this creates another social, psychological problem in what we like to refer to as a subculture, which is a part of the bill which the country's going to have to pay.

I'm thinking . . .

Bills always do come in; one always has to pay.

There's always a . . . there's a phrase Sandburg uses: "Slums always seek their revenge." In other ways, they do, too.

Yes, they do; yes, they do indeed.

I'm thinking about the matriarchal setup of the Negro family, the Negro life. Even back in the slave days, the underground railway leaders, Harriet Tubman, were the women.

Yeah, yeah. It's a terrible thing. Negro women have, for generations, raised white children, who sometimes lynched their children, and tried to raise their child like a man, and yet in the full knowledge that if he really walks around like a man, he's going to be cut down. It's a terrible kind of dilemma. It's a terrible price to ask anybody to pay. And in this country Negro women have been paying it for three hundred years, and for a hundred of those years, when they were legally and technically free.

When people talk about time, therefore, you know, I really can't help but be absolutely, not only impatient, but bewildered. Why should I wait any longer? And in any case, even if I were willing to—which I'm not—*how?*

The point, you mean, about go slow.

Go slow. Yes.

Go slow; take it easy. Again, there's a last sentence you have in the Faulkner chapter about how a change—about whatever approach to humanity, to being human beings—it must be now. The moment, you speak of—

It's always now.

The world we're living in. We have to make it over, the world we live in. We made the world we live in, but you speak of now; it's always now.

Time is always now. I think everybody who's thought about his own life knows this. You know you don't make resolutions about something you're going to do next year. No. You decide to write a book? No. The book may be finished twenty years from now, but you've got to start it now.

I'm thinking of the subtitle of your book and the position of the Negro woman–Negro man—Notes of a Native Son. *Naturally, I immediately think of Richard Wright, who has meant so much to you as an artist and as a man.*

Yes, yes, yes, yes.

And his short story, you refer to this beautifully here in the chapter "Alas Poor Richard"—one of the three chapters on Richard Wright—"Man of All Work," in which the husband, to get a job, dresses himself up in his wife's clothes and hires himself as a cook.

Yeah. It's a beautiful, terrifying story. And it really gets at something which has been hidden for all these generations, which is the ways in which— It really suggests, more forcibly than anything I've read, really, the humiliation the Negro man endures. And it's this which the country doesn't want to know.

And therefore, when people talk about the "noble savage," you know, and the greater sexuality of Negroes and all that jazz, you know— Whereas I know I could name, if we were not on the air, six people who I know, with whom I grew up, six men who are on the needle, just because there is really no . . . the demoralization is so complete. In order to make the act of love, there's got to be a certain confidence, a certain trust. Otherwise it degenerates into nothing but desperate and featureless brutality.

You've spoken of the needle now, and we think, of course, of junkies and we think of narcotics, and here again, perhaps for some the only means of escape from the brutal reality.

Yes, that's right. That's right. I knew a boy very well once, who told me, almost in just that many words, that he wasn't trying to get high he was just trying to hold himself together, you know. He also said, talking about himself walking through one of our cities one morning and the way people looked at him . . . And he said to himself, he told me: You ought to be able to bear me if I can bear you.

What is most appalling about it is that all of these things might not be so terrible if, when facing well-meaning white people, one didn't realize that they don't know anything about this at all and don't want to know. And this, somehow, really is the last drop in a very bitter cup. Because if *they* don't know and don't want to know, then what hope is there?

When people talk to me about the strides that have been made and—all these dreary movies Hollywood keeps turning out about be kind to Negroes today, and isn't this a good sign, well, of course they've never seen these movies with a Negro audience watching them.

What is the reaction?

Well, for example, in *The Defiant Ones*, a movie which I really cannot say anything about. [Laughs] At the end of that movie, when Sidney, who was very brilliant in it, and who does his best with a rather dreary role—there's something with it which I wouldn't believe could have been done. Anyway, at the end of that movie, when Sidney jumps off that train to rescue Tony Curtis— Downtown, I saw it twice deliberately. I saw it down-town in front of a white, liberal audience—I suppose they're liberal—there was a great sigh of relief and clapping, and I felt that this was a very noble gesture on the part of a very noble black man. And I suppose in a way it was.

I saw it uptown, and Sidney jumps off the train, and there's a tremendous roar of fury from the audience, with which I must say I agreed, you know. They told Sidney to "get back on the train, you fool." And in any case, why would he go back to the chain gang when they're obviously going to be separated again?—a silly Jim Crow chain gang. What's the movie supposed to prove? What the movie is designed to prove really, to white people, is that Negroes are going to forgive them for their crimes, and that somehow they're going to escape scot-free.

Now, I myself am not being vengeful when I say this at all, because I would hate to see the nightmare begin all over again with the shoe on the other foot. But I'm talking about a human fact, and the human fact is this: that one can't escape anything that one's done. One's got to pay for it. And you either pay for it willingly or you pay for it unwillingly.

As you say this—and I was thinking of the Negro audience, and "get back on the train, you fool"—we think of two movements happening simultaneously with the Negro in America today: the black Muslim movement and Martin Luther King. And here it seems to be directly connected, doesn't it?

Yes, precisely. And I must admit that there is a great ambivalence in myself. For example, I'm devoted to King and I've worked with CORE and tried to raise money for the freedom riders. And I adore those children; I have tremendous respect for them. And yet, at the same time, in talking to very different people, and somewhat older, and also talking to excellent students who said I simply can't take it anymore . . . I don't know.

Let me put it another way. King's influence is tremendous, but his influence in the North is slight. And the North doesn't talk about the South. Chicagoans talk about Mississippi as though they had no South Side, and, you know, white people in New York talk about Alabama as though they had no Harlem. And it's a great device on the part of white people to ignore what's happening in their own backyard. Now whether, let us say, I were for or against violence, this is absolutely irrelevant.

The question which really obsesses me today is that whether or not I like it, and whether or not you like it, unless this situation is ameliorated, and very, very quickly, there will *be* violence. There will be violence—and I am as convinced of this as I am that I'm sitting in this chair—one day in Birmingham. And it won't be the fault of the Negroes in Birmingham; it's the fault of the administration in Birmingham and the apathy of Washington. It is an intolerable situation, which has been intolerable for one hundred years.

I really cannot tell my nephew or my brother—my nephew is fourteen; my brother is a grown man—I can't really tell my nephew that when someone hits him he shouldn't hit back. I really cannot tell him that. Still less can I tell my brother that if someone comes to his house with a gun he should let him in— no—and allow him to do what he wants with his children and his wife. But the point is, even if I *were* able to tell my brother that he should, there's absolutely no guarantee that my brother will, and I can't blame him.

It's too easy, in another way, for the country to sit in admiration before the sit-in students, because it doesn't cost them anything. And they have no idea what it costs those kids to go through that, to picket a building, for example, when people upstairs in the building are spitting down on your head or trying to vomit down on you. This is a tremendous amount to demand of people who are technically free, in a free country, which is supposed to be the leader of the West. It seems to me a great cowardice on the part of the public to expect that it's going to be saved by a handful of children for whom they refuse to be responsible.

And so it is so much more difficult, then, so much more easy, I should say, for a black Muslim speaker to win followers than for Martin Luther King, who is asking so much.

It is always much easier, obviously, to . . . How can I put this? Well, in Harlem, there are meetings every Saturday night; those people are there, listening to those speeches and all kinds of other speeches, because they are in despair, and they don't believe. And this is the most dangerous thing that has happened. They don't believe. They've been betrayed so often and by so many people, not all of them white, they don't believe that the country really means what it says, and there is nothing in the record to indicate the country means what it says.

Now, when they're told that they are better than white people, it is a perfectly inevitable development. You know, if for all these hundreds of years white people are going around saying that they're better than anybody else, sooner or later they're bound to create a counterweight to this, especially with Africa on the stage of the world now, which is simply to take the whole legend of Western history, the entire theology, changing one or two pronouns, and transferring from Jerusalem to Islam, and just this small change can turn it all against the white world. And the white world can't do anything about this, can't call the Muslim leaders or anybody else on this, until they're willing to face their own history.

How does all this then connect with a Negro artist, a Negro writer, specifically you, coming out, and to a man who meant so much to you, Richard

Wright? That is, again, coming back to Wright's chapter, he escaped. He spoke of Paris as a refuge, but you looked upon it as a sort of way station for yourself.

Well, in the beginning, I looked upon Paris as a refuge, too; I never intended to come back to this country.

I lived there so long, though, and I got to know a great deal about Paris, and I suppose that several things happened to me. One of them was watching American Negroes there who had dragged Mississippi, so to speak, across the ocean with them, and are operating now in a vacuum. I myself, you know, carried all my social habits to Paris with me, where they were not needed, where it took me a long time to learn how to do without them. And this complex frightened me very much.

But more important than that, perhaps, was my relationship with Africans and with Algerians there who belonged to France, and it didn't demand any spectacularly great perception to realize that I was treated, insofar as I was noticed at all, differently from them because I had an American passport. I may not have liked this fact, but it was a fact. And I could see very well that if I were an Algerian I would not have been living in the same city in which I imagined myself to be living as Jimmy Baldwin. Or if I were an African, it would have been a very different city for me. And I also began to see that the West, the entire West, was changing, was breaking up; that its power over me, over Africans, was gone and would never come again. So then it seemed that exile was but another way of being in limbo.

But I suppose, finally, the most important thing was that I am a writer, and that sounds grandiloquent, but the truth is that I don't think that, seriously speaking, anybody in his right mind would want to be a writer. But you do discover that you are one, and then you haven't got any choice; either you live that life or you don't live any. And I'm an American writer; this country is my subject. And in working out the forthcoming novel, I began to realize that the New York I was trying to describe was a New York that was by this time nearly twenty years old. I had to come back to check my impressions and to, as it turned out, to be stung again, to look at it again, bear it again, and be reconciled to it again.

Now, I imagine, in my own case, I will have to spend the rest of my life, however long that will be, as a kind of transatlantic commuter. Because at some point when I'm in this country I always get to a place where I realize I don't see it very clearly anymore. Because it's very exhausting to spend—after all, you do spend twenty-four hours a day resisting and resenting it, you know, and trying to keep a kind of equilibrium in it. So I suppose that I will keep going away and coming back.

You feel your years in Europe afforded you more of a perspective?

Yeah. I began to see this country for the first time. If I hadn't gone away, I would never have been able to see it, and if I hadn't been able to see it, I would never have been able to forgive it.

You know, I'm not mad at this country anymore. I'm very worried about it. And I'm not worried about the Negroes in the country even so much as I'm worried about the country. The country doesn't know what it's done to Negroes. But the country has no notion whatever—and this is disastrous—about what it's done to itself. They have yet to assess the price they paid, North and South, for keeping the Negro in his place. And, from my point of view, it shows in every single level of our lives, from the most public—

Could you expand on this a little, Jim, on what the country has done to itself?

Well, one of the reasons, for example, I think that our youth is so badly educated—and it is inconceivably badly educated—is because education demands a certain daring, a certain independence of mind. You have to teach young people to think, and in order to teach young people to think, you have to teach them to think about everything. There mustn't be something they cannot think about. If there's one thing they can't think about, then very shortly they can't think about anything, you know.

Now, there's always something in this country, of course, that one cannot think about, and what one cannot think about is the Negro. Now, this may seem like a very subtle argument, but I don't think so. I think that really time will prove the connection between the level of the lives we lead, and this extraordinary endeavor to avoid black men. And I think it shows in our public life.

When I was living in Europe, it occurred to me that what Americans in Europe did not know about Europeans is precisely what they didn't know about me. And what Americans today don't know about the rest of the world, like Cuba, or Africa, is what they don't know about me. An incoherent—totally incoherent—foreign policy of this country is a reflection of the incoherence of the private lives here.

So we don't even know our own names.

No, we don't. That's the whole point. And I suggest this: that in order to learn your name, you're going to have to learn mine.

In a way, the American Negro is the key figure in this country. And if we don't face him, we will never face anything.

If I don't know your name, I, a white man, will never know mine. Thinking now, as a country—We think of Africa immediately, and you have, again (returning to your work, by the way, may I suggest this work to listeners—James Baldwin's. Nobody Knows My Name, *published by Dial, and even though I say it is a collection of essays, it isn't that. It is a novel; it is an autobiography, really, in a way), you have a journalistic report, and a very accurate and astute one: "Princes and Powers," it's called. You were covering a meeting of Negro writers of the world in Paris, and African writers were speaking, too.*

Yeah. It was really an African conference; it was predominantly African. The Negroes were there as Africans, or as, well, the black people of the world, let's put it that way.

What of the African writer, then? You mentioned Wole here. Isn't there a problem here? The uncovering of this rich heritage, so long buried, by kidnappers, by colonial people. And at the same time we know that technological advances are taking place, changes, the slums are being cleared—

The twentieth century, in fact—

Now isn't there loss as well as gain here? It's a question of things happening at the same time.

It's a very great question. It's almost impossible to assess what was lost, which makes it impossible to assess what's gained. How can I put this? In a way, I almost envy African writers because there's so much to excavate, you know, and because their relationship to the world, at least from my vantage point—and about this I may be wrong—seems much more direct than mine can ever be. But God knows, the colonial experience destroyed so much, blasted so much, and of course changed forever the African personality. So one doesn't know what really was there on the other side of the flood. It's going to take generations before that past can be reestablished and, in effect, used.

And at the same time, of course, all of the African nations are under the obligation, the necessity, of moving into the twentieth century at really some fantastic rate of speed, which is the only way they can survive. And of course all Africans, whether they know it or not, have endured the European experience and have been stained and changed by the European standards.

In a curious way, the unification of Africa, insofar as it can be said to exist, is a white invention. That is to say, the only thing that really unites, as far as I can tell, all black men everywhere, is the fact that white men are on their necks. What I'm curious about is what will happen when this is no longer true and for the first time in the memory of anybody living, black men have their destinies in their own hands. What will come out then, and what the problems and tensions and terrors will be then, is a very great and very loaded question.

I think that if we were more honest here we could do a great deal to aid in this transition. Because we have an advantage, which we certainly consider to be a disadvantage, over all the other Western nations. That is to say, we have created—forgetting, you know, quite apart from anything else—the fact is we have created, and no other nation has, a black man who belongs, who is a part of the West. Now, and in distinction to Belgium or any other European power, we had our slaves on the mainland. And therefore, no matter how we deny it, we couldn't avoid human involvement with them, which we've almost perished denying, but which is, nevertheless, there.

Now, if we could turn about and face this, we could have a tremendous advantage in the world today. But as long as we don't, there isn't much hope for the West, really. If one can accept the fact that it is no longer important to be white, it would begin to cease to be important to be black. If one could accept the fact that no nation with twenty million black people in it, for so long and with such depth of involvement—no nation under these circumstances can really be called a white nation, this would be a great achievement and it would change a great many things.

This raises a very interesting point. This is all conjecture, of course, assuming that sanity is maintained, assuming that humanity itself, the humanity in all of us, will triumph. Just as you say there will be no white nation and no black nation, but nations of people, now we come to a question of this long, varied heritage.

At the beginning, a Bessie Smith record was played. You, once upon a time, not knowing who you were, were ashamed of it, and now realize there's a great pride here in artistry. I'm thinking now of the young African. Again, if a certain identity, and this is an imposed identity from the outside, is lost, will he reject that which was uniquely his for a grayness, perhaps? Even though it be more materially advanced?

I have a tendency to doubt it, but then of course there's no way of knowing. I have a tendency, judging only from my very limited experience in Paris with a few Africans after all—my tendency is to doubt it.

I think that the real impulse is to excavate that heritage, at no matter what cost, and bring it into the present. And I think that this is a very sound idea, because I think it's needed. I think that all the things that were destroyed by Europe, which will never really be put in place again, still in that rubble I think there's something of very great value, not only for Africans, but for all of us.

I really think that we're living in a moment which is as important as that moment when Constantine became a Christian. I think that all the standards by which the Western world has lived for so long are in the process of breakdown and of revision, and a kind of passion and a kind of beauty and a kind of joy which was in the world before, and has been buried so long, has got to come back.

The passion and beauty and joy once in the world have been buried. Now we come to the matter of dehumanization, don't we?

Yes, exactly.

The impersonality of our times.

Yes, yes, yes. And obviously this cannot— Well, I would hate to see it continue. I don't ever intend to make my peace with such a world.

There's something much more important than Cadillacs, Frigidaires, and IBM machines. And precisely one of the things wrong with this country is this notion that IBM machines and Cadillacs prove something. People are always telling me how many Negroes bought Cadillacs last year, and it terrifies me. I always wonder: Is this what you think the country is for? And do you think this is really what I came here and suffered and died for? A lousy Cadillac?

Whether it's for white or black, is this what our country's for?

For white or black, yes, exactly. I think the country's got to find out what it means by "freedom." Freedom is a very dangerous thing, you know. Anything else is disastrous. But freedom is dangerous. You know, you've got to make choices; you've got to make very dangerous choices; you've got to be taught that your life is in your hands.

A matter of freedom. This leads to another chapter in your book dealing with your meeting with Ingmar Bergman, whom you described as a relatively free artist. Would you mind telling us a bit about that, what you meant by that?

Well, part of his freedom, of course, is just purely economical. It's based on the social structure, the economic structure of Sweden. So he hasn't got to worry about the money for his films, which is a very healthy thing for him.

But on another level, he impressed me as being free because he had—and this is a great paradox, it seems to me, about freedom—because he had accepted his limitations, the limitations within himself and the limitations within his society. I don't mean that he necessarily accepted these limitations; I don't mean that he was passive in the face of them. But he'd recognized that he was Ingmar Bergman who could do some things, and therefore could not do some others. He was not going to live forever. He had recognized what people in this country have a great deal of trouble recognizing, that life is very difficult, very difficult for *anybody*, anybody born. Now, I don't think people can be free until they recognize this.

In the same way Bessie Smith was much freer—always and

terrible as this may sound—much freer than the people who murdered her, or let her die, you know. And Big Bill Broonzy was a much freer man than the success-ridden people running around on Madison Avenue today. If you can accept the worst, as someone said to me, then you can see the best. But if you think life is a great big, glorious plum pudding, you'll end up in the madhouse, which is where, you know . . .

To perhaps even extend the examples you just offered: the little girl who walked into the Little Rock schoolhouse, or the Charlotte, North Carolina, schoolhouse, and was spat on was much freer than the white child who sat there with a misconceived notion.

Yes, yes, exactly. Well, I think the proof that Negroes are much stronger in the South today is simply, you know—

She knew who she was.

She knew who she was. And after all, that child has been coming for a very long time. She didn't come out of nothing. That Negro families are able to produce such children, whereas the good white people of the South have yet to make any appearance, proves something awful about the moral state of the South. Those people in Tallahassee who are never in the streets when the mobs are there, well, you know, why aren't they? It's their town, too.

What about someone like Lillian Smith? *

* Lillian Smith, a liberal white woman in a Georgia town, who alone challenged the community to treat black people as fellow humans. She was threatened, daily, but in no way gave in. Her most celebrated novel was *Strange Fruit.*

Lillian Smith is a great—I think a very great—and heroic, and very lonely figure, obviously. She has very few friends in that little hamlet in Georgia where she carries on so gallantly. She's paid a tremendous price for trying to do what she thinks is right. And the price *is* terribly, terribly high. The only way for the price to become a little less is for more people to pay it.

Of course, here is someone of the South, a minority of one, and perhaps there are a few prototypes here and there. This leads to the—I'm looking through your book now, and I feel guilty for not having finished it before interviewing you. I'm sure you have something about majority-minority, perhaps, about the majority is not necessarily right all the time.

The majority is usually—I hate to say this—wrong. I think there's a great confusion in this country anyway about that.

Ibsen's Enemy of the People.

Yes, yes. I really think seriously there's a division of labor in the world. And some people are here to, I can see . . . Let me put it this way: There are so many things I'm not good at. I can't drive a truck. I couldn't run a bank. Well, all right. Other people have to do that. Well, in a way they're responsible to me and I'm responsible to them, you know.

My responsibility to them is to try to tell the truth as I see it—not so much about my private life as about *their* private lives, you know. So that there is in the world a standard for *all* of us, which will get you through your trouble. Because your trouble's always coming, you know. And Cadillacs don't get you through it. And neither do psychiatrists, incidentally. All that gets you through it, really, is some faith in life, which is not so easy to achieve.

Now, when you talk about majorities and minorities, I always have the feeling that this country's talking about a kind of popularity contest in which everybody works together toward some absolutely hideous, hideously material end. But in truth, I think that politicians—for example, in the South where it's shown most clearly—I think all the southern politicians have failed their responsibility to the white people of the South. Somebody in the South must know that obviously the situation, the status quo, will not exist another hundred years. And their responsibility is to prepare the people who are now forming those mobs, to prepare those people for that day. You know, to minimize the damage to *them*, even.

Now, the majority rule in the South is not a majority rule at all; it's a mob rule. And what these mobs feel is a moral vacuum, which is created by the lack of a leader. And it seems to me this is the way the world is. And I'm not talking about dictatorships. I mean that—

Statesmen.

Statesmen, and people who are sitting in government are supposed to know more about government than people who are driving trucks and digging potatoes and trying to raise their children. That's what you're in the office for.

Someone, then, with a sense of history, perhaps.

Yes, which is precisely what we don't have here.

Sense of history.

Yes, if you don't know what's happened behind you, you have no idea what's happening around you. That's a law.

Earlier, Jim, you mentioned that for a national policy to be straightened out, the private policies, the private lives, the individual lives, must be.

That's right.

And you spoke, too, of your job as a writer; you've got to write. And in this chapter with Bergman, "The Northern Protestant," there's a beautiful comment here: "All art is a kind of confession, more or less oblique. All artists, if they're to survive, are forced at last to tell the whole story, to vomit the anguish up. All of it, the literal and the fanciful." Of whom you speak, of Bergman. But all art is a kind of confession, as you apparently do in all your writings.

I think it has to be a kind of confession. I don't mean a true confession in the sense of that dreary magazine. But I mean the effort seems to me is to— If you can examine and face your life, you can discover the terms in which you're connected to other lives, and they can discover, too, the terms in which they're connected to other people.

It's happened to every one of us, I'm sure, that one has read something which you thought only happened to you and you discover that it happened a hundred years ago to Dostoyevsky. And this is a very great liberation for the suffering, struggling person who always thinks that he's alone. This is why it's important.

Art would not be important if life were not more important. And life is important. And life is . . . Mainly, most of us, no matter what we say, are walking in the dark, whistling in the dark. Nobody knows what's going to happen to him from one moment to the next or how he will bear it. And this is irreducible, and it's true for everybody.

Now, it is true that the nature of society has to be to create, among its citizens, an illusion of safety. But it's also absolutely true that the safety is always necessarily an illusion, and artists are here to disturb the peace.

Artists are here to disturb the peace.

Yes. They have to disturb the peace; otherwise, chaos.

Life is risk.

It is indeed; it is. It always is. It always is. And people have to know this. Some way they have to know it in order to get through their risks.

So the safety itself is wholly illusory.

Yes. There's no such a thing as safety on this planet. No one knows that much. No one ever will—let alone about the world, but about himself. That's why of course it's unsafe. And people in some way have to know this. And this is what the whole sense of tragedy is really all about. And people think, I think, that a sense of tragedy is a kind of embroidery, or something irrelevant which you can take or leave. But in fact, it's a necessity. That's what the blues are all about. That's what spirituals are about. It is the ability to look on things as they are and survive your losses. Or even not survive them, but to know that they're coming. Because knowing they're coming is the only possible insurance you have, some faint insurance, that you will survive them.

You spoke of a sense of tragedy. Again, in your book, you speak of us Americans lacking. We have tremendous potentialities, but you're saying that we lack that which a non-American may have, a sense of tragedy.

Yes, I think we do, and it's incredible to me that—and I'm not trying to oversimplify anything—but it is incredible to me that in this country, where, after all, materially, for the most part, one is better off than anywhere else in the world, that one should know so many people who are in a state of the most absolute insecurity about themselves. So they literally can't get through a morning without going to see the psychiatrist. And I find it very difficult to take this really seriously, since other people who have really terrifying and unimaginable troubles, from the American point of view, don't dream of going anywhere near a psychiatrist and wouldn't have the money to do it if they were mad enough to dream it.

It seems to me it points to a very great, well, not illness exactly, but fear. Frenchmen that I used to know, Frenchwomen, spend much less time in this dreadful internal warfare, tearing themselves and each other to pieces, than Americans do. And why this is so is probably a question for someone else. But it is so, and I think it says something very serious about the real aims and the real standards of our society. People don't live by the standards they say they live by. And the gap between their profession and the actuality is what creates this despair and this uncertainty, which is very, very dangerous.

In the last chapter, the last part of your book Nobody Knows My Name, *the black boy looks at the white boy—it's your relationship to Norman Mailer—but the very last part says if he has understood them, then he is richer; he, in this instance, the white boy. "Then he is richer and we are richer, too; if he has not understood them, we are all much poorer. For though it clearly needs to be brought into focus, he has a real vision of ourselves as we are, and it cannot be too often repeated in this country now that where there is no vision, the people perish."*

Mmm-hmm. I mean that.

And the hour has gone so ludicrously rapidly. James Baldwin, who has confessed, in a very beautiful way. But the confession, here, is most brief. We merely scratched the surface in slightly knowing James Baldwin.

Perhaps, one last question, James Baldwin. Who are you now?

Who, indeed! Well, I may not be able to tell you quite who I am, but I think I'm discovering who I'm not. I want to be an honest man, and I want to be a good writer. [A pause] And I don't know if one ever gets to be what one wants to be. I think you just have to play it by ear and pray for rain.

"CITY OF HANDS WAS BORN IN MUD AND FIRE," *FINANCIAL TIMES*, 2005

CHICAGO. Where shall we begin? For years the impression of Chicago in a popular sense, thanks to Warner Bros. movies, was Jimmy Cagney, Edward G. Robinson—Chicago was the home of the mob, Al Capone.

The name Al Capone and Chicago were at times synonymous, and Chicago was a tough, rough city.

Its beginnings were swampland, the Potawatomi Indians, who were pretty well scalped financially by the pirates who we call our Founding Fathers and after whom streets are named.

And Nelson Algren, a Chicago writer years ago, a great critic of Chicago in a very lyrical way, wrote *The Man with the Golden Arm*, *The Neon Wilderness*; he wrote a book called *Chicago: City on the Make*. It's like a prose poem.

Chicago began with French *voyageurs*, and then the Germans came. Many were liberal Germans. In terms of the '48ers—1848, you know, was the year of many rebellions, all of which failed, and so Chicago had a sort of liberal, to some extent,

German tradition. You find that in the arts. For example, the Chicago Symphony [Orchestra] was primarily Teutonic—Brahms, Beethoven, Bach.

At the same time, Chicago became what I call the key, archetypical American city—a blue-collar city. Not a New York, New Orleans, or San Francisco. There's a glamour attached to each. Chicago never had that glamour, but it had something else.

It had a resettlement and reform program with Jane Addams, a social worker; she was the first in our country to have a settlement idea. She established Hull-House for a lot of the Italian immigrants.

So Chicago's reputation on one side was Al Capone and on the other side was Jane Addams.

It also was a city of the blue collar because after the Germans came the Irish, of course, and the Irish had an advantage; they spoke English. So they became part of the political scene for a long time.

But the big thing about Chicago was the hands—"city of hands." It's an old-fashioned phrase for workers: "50 hands wanted." In John Steinbeck's *Of Mice and Men*, George and Lenny go down to skid row, and they see all kinds of guys with signs saying "50 hands wanted." Chicago, city of hands—all these immigrants from Eastern Europe.

Chicago's Polish population was at one time the biggest in the world with the exception of Warsaw's. Then came the Mediterranean migration; then, of course, since then, the Mexicans and Latino people have come.

And of course the inner migration—the Deep South of the United States, the black people who as sharecroppers heard about Chicago. The big newspaper among black people for years was *The Defender*—carried by the Pullman car porters. They were the aristocrats, when they came into a poolroom, or a barbershop or a restaurant, with their blue pants and their white stripes. They were carrying *The Defender*, which would give them news of the rest of the world—especially Chicago.

In fact there's a blues song by Jimmy Rushing—he used to sing with Count Basie—he'd sing "Gone to Chicago, baby, sorry I can't take you." Chicago became the home for many black people because here were the steel mills, the packing houses.

Chicago was also a railroad center—a thousand trains a day would pass through and stop in Chicago. I remember coming here in 1920 as a little kid. My parents had a rooming house here. My father was ill. I remember coming on a train. Oh, it was exciting. Chicago: home of the skyscrapers.

So Chicago was unique; it was the archetypical American city. It had these immigrants who did the hard work and the labor in all these steel and farm-equipment plants. Actually every city had its uniqueness then. You'd get off the train and see this was Pittsburgh or this was Detroit. There'd be some landmark.

Today you get off a plane. What do you see? The Red Lobster [restaurant chain]. The Golden Arches. Marriott hotels. You can't tell one city from another. This actually happened to me. I write these books called oral histories. In the past, I'd travel around on book tours. And so I'd go to maybe ten cities by plane, and so one day I'm in this city—and remember you can't tell one city from the next—and I'm at this motel and I say to the switchboard operator: "Could you ring me at six o'clock in the morning because I've got to be in Cleveland by eight?" And she says: "Sir, you *are* in Cleveland."

That's how Chicago's changed. Of course, it's a change for all cities, the sameness. Cities have lost their uniqueness, their individuality.

All cities have neighborhoods, but the word has a special meaning to Chicago because of its Germans, the Irish; now we have Asians as well. Chicago's known for its "two-flats" buildings: two apartments. One [owned] by some worker who'd saved his money and, up above, his son-in-law and his daughter. That was a big pattern—a family in two-flat bungalows. In New York there'd be tenements. A lot have become gentrified, but there are still these neighborhoods, good and bad.

*   *   *

Chicago was also the home of some of labor's most bloody battles. There was Gene Debs, fighting to organize the railroad unions, fiercely battling against the Pullman Palace Car Company. Pullman organized the ideal town for his good honest workman. No Irish allowed. The Irish were the blacks of their day. It was said of the Irish: coal in the bathtub, promiscuous, living on the dole—all the earmarks stereotypically associated with black people. That was a battle.

And of course there was 1886, the fight for an eight-hour workday. The first time that phrase was ever used anywhere in the world was in Chicago when local anarchists and others gathered to campaign for it. There was a meeting. The rains came heavily. The speakers went home, the mayor, Carter Harrison, a good man, was there on horseback and saw that all was quiet. Most of the crowd had dispersed when someone, we don't even know who, threw a bomb. It killed several police officers and some laymen. The hysterical headlines of the local papers all said: "Hang Them!" The case caused indignation the world over, from Leo Tolstoy to Mahatma Gandhi to George Bernard Shaw.

Several enlightened industrialists were for commuting the sentence. But the merchant prince, Marshall Field I, with his white mustache pointing heavenward, said, "Hang the Bastards!" and they did.

There was also 1937, the Memorial Day Massacre, when the strikers of Republic Steel Company gathered for a mass meeting. The weather was fine; it was a perfect day for a picnic. Men brought their wives and children for a parade and mass rally. But five hundred policemen were stationed there, fully armed with guns loaded with real bullets. As the marchers, singing, made their way toward the plant, the cops began whaling away with their billy clubs. Panic. And then the cops started shooting. Ten men were shot in the back. Killed. Over a hundred wounded. There were strikes by the score in Chicago.

As for the black man, great as the opportunities were at the time for jobs, especially in the stockyards, the black man found few openings. Even Lake Michigan was divided. A young black kid happened to swim past the invisible division line. He was shot and killed, sparking the race riot of 1919. Martin Luther King Jr. visiting Chicago made an astonishing discovery: that where he had traveled was more dangerous than Birmingham and Bull Connor's dogs. A rock struck Dr. King and left him with a bruise as a fond keepsake of Chicago.

So there you have it. Chicago's god is Janus of two faces. The one that says come on here, there are jobs, all hands wanted. And the other that says, not you, *you* stay away.

JANUS: SOME PORTRAITS FROM MEMORY

IT WAS THE MOST SEGREGATED of all northern cities. You must understand that our god is different from all others. We worship Janus, the two-faced deity. There is a full human being here, his sunny and his dark side: his life-liness and his necrophia. Former governor George Ryan, imprisoned in a state penitentiary for malfeasance in office, is a likely candidate for the Nobel Peace Prize. He struck the first blow against capital punishment and cleaned out the death cell allowing the condemned a new trial on the basis of the DNA evidence. Some who were due to be executed were freed, innocent of any crime.

Harold Washington was to become our first black Mayor in the country's most segregated northern city. After an unprecedented brutal campaign, he was easily reelected. A great many white voters were impressed that the trains ran on time and the garbage was picked up regularly.

Let's continue with Janus, the god of two faces. I worked with both sides of that Janus. One was my raffish colleague Vincent De Paul Garrity and the other was my sound engineer Frank Tuller. They represented all of Janus I needed to know, Chicago clout and innocents.

Vince Garrity, 1974

SQUINTY-EYED THROUGH THICK-LENSED GLASSES. Short, squat, with intimations of a potbelly. No Robert Redford, this one. So what? He was a celebrity in his hometown. It's what he had in mind from the very first: that summer night so long, long ago—was it 1937?—when he, a face in the crowd, hopped onto the running board of FDR's open car as it came off the Outer Drive, newly built and dedicated. Sure, the Secret Service men handled him roughly. At first. Then they came to know him. And who didn't? As he wistfully recalled: "I thought it was time the president met Vincent De Paul Garrity."

Sure, he was batboy for the Cubs. But that wasn't it. Sure, he was office boy to Big Ed Kelly, the Daley of the day. But that wasn't it. God Almighty, he even knew Walter Winchell. But that wasn't it, either.

Every man is Parsifal, seeking the Holy Grail. For Vince, *to be known* was not quite the ultimate meaning of life, but it was close enough. He went along with Ecclesiastes: To everything there is a purpose under Heaven. To be known for its own sake was not quite what this pilgrim, traveling through this world of woe, had in mind. Any clod seen often enough on the tube or heard over the airwaves, day to day, can achieve that. Consider Zsa Zsa Gabor, Merv Griffin, Howard Miller, or any humpty-dumpty, Mr. or Mrs., you'd care to name. Any clod can achieve that through well-publicized scandal. Consider Clifford Irving. Any clod can make it truly big as a "world statesman" in this nutty society, fused to a sudden, crazy event thousands of miles away: the Sino-Soviet Era of Hard Feeling.

Consider Henry Kissinger, Peter Sellers's most deadly deft mimic.

No, what Vince had in mind was wholly something else. He was determined to be known to every cop, every ambulance chaser, every city hall coat holder, as well as those whose coats were held, every hood, no matter how large or small his enterprise, every judge (not Supreme Court member, no, no, none o' that; just the hardworking pie card, whose hard work—bringing in the sheaves—landed him, by virtue of this virtue, on the municipal court bench instead of in the defendant's dock) and the sundry other worthies who have helped make this Frank Sinatra's kind of town. And he was so known.

Unlike most red-blooded American boys, Vince did not want to grow up to be president. He didn't even want to be mayor. All he wanted to be was another Paddy Nash, "the power behind the t'rone" in the days of Big Ed. Not in Washington, D.C. No, no, none o' that. Just here, in the true Fat City, bearing a wild Potawatomi name. His devout wish was to be known for one glory purpose: to be the ultimate clout on his own turf. And in some wondrous cockeyed way, he succeeded. At least in one memorable instance.

Much has been written of the 1968 Democratic convention in Chicago. And the Big Dumpling's lack of élan. Little has been written of the 1952 Republican Convention in Chicago. And the Little Dumpling's exquisite display of élan. Vince De Paul Garrity admired Richard J. Daley, as Little invariably admires Big. Yet, the worshipped, in this instance, was much more hip to the religion of clout than his idol. By a country mile.

Historians, political scientists, and distinguished journalists may have written about that convention. But what do they know of the way of the world? Did Teddy White chronicle that one, too? Dusty, dull, and pedestrian, all of them. What do they know of the comic art of clout? What do they know of the fine and lively art of Vincent De Paul Garrity?

To begin. Red Quinlan, the most original and imaginative of Chicago television executives, was, at the time, station manager of WBKB, an affiliate of ABC. Derring-do was Red's most singular and endearing attribute. While TV executives, not just here but throughout our promised land, were ciphers, superfluous in swivel chairs, Red risked. He made errors, the kind a wide-ranging shortstop, say Marty Marion, was impelled to make. Hiring Vince for this one occasion was not one of them.

To refresh the memories of those old enough—and to offer unrecorded history for the newer people, who assume the world began with themselves—the American Broadcasting Company won every award in the books—Peabodies and et ceteras—for its coverage of the 1952 convention. Its most celebrated recipients were John Daly and Martin Agronsky, the commentators. Know who *really* won it for ABC, though he was, of course, accorded no such recognition? Vince. He was truly "the power behind the t'rone."

An explanation is in order. Red Q decided to put Vince on the ABC payroll for the express purpose of easing the way for the network's visiting firemen, whose faces and voices were so familiar on the TV screen, but who knew from zero about the city they were visiting. Vince knew, not in spades, perhaps, but in blue. He knew every cop who stood guard at the amphitheater, the convention's arena. What's more to the point, they all knew him.

So it was Vince who advised the officer at the press gate or mass media gate, or whatever it was called: "Watch me for the high sign. If I shake my head, don't let 'em in. Got it?"

"Got it, Vince. Whatever you say."

It came to pass that H. V. Kaltenborn, NBC's most renowned pundit, accompanied by his producer and assorted gofers, was barreling toward the gate in an NBC special limousine. As is the wont of such Eastern hotshots working the benighted hinterlands, the air was one of towering confidence and, by its very nature, of cool contempt toward the natives. A card was flashed, en passant. But the Red Sea did not part. The cop said, "Just a minute."

"We're NBC," somebody said, clarion clear.

"I said just a minute."

The officer turned away. He was peering, it appeared, at somebody several yards distant. Somebody short, squat, and squinty-eyed. He waited for a sign. After what seemed an appropriate passage of time, the mysterious figure slowly, and with an air of dolor, shook its head.

"Sorry," murmured the man in uniform. "Can't get in."

"Are you crazy?" A caterwaul in Manhattan nasal. "We're the National Broadcasting Company! And that's *H. V. Kaltenborn* back there!"

"I don't care if it's Gabby Hartnett. Ya can't get in."

"We *must*! He's got an important interview with Senator Taft's campaign manager. Can't you read our credentials? N—B—C!"

"I can read. Move to one side, please."

Another limo was pulling in. Again, the indolent, languorous flash of a card.

"Just a minute."

"Just a minute? We're *CBS*!"

The gentleman in blue turned away. Again, he peered toward the short, squat, squinty-eyed body several yards distant. After what seemed an appropriate passage of time, the mysterious figure slowly, and with an air of dolor, shook its head.

"Sorry. Ya can't get in."

"Are you crazy?" Another caterwaul—this one in Scarsdale nasal.

"We're the *Columbia Broadcasting System*. Do you know who's sitting back there? *Ed Murrow and Eric Sevareid*!"

"I don't care if it's Luke Appling and Art Shires. Ya can't get in."

"We *must*! We've got an important interview with Eisenhower's campaign manager. Can't you read our credentials? *C—B—S*!"

"I can read. Move to one side, please."

Another important-looking car was pulling in. Again, a card flashed. The policeman turned away. Once more, he looked for guidance. This time, the short, squat, squinty-eyed man of mystery nodded. Determinedly, quickly.

"Okay, sir. Sorry for the delay."

The car whizzed by.

Thus it was that ABC scooped its two rivals, again and again and again, during that remarkable convention of 1952. And it was duly honored with plaques and plenty of adulatory ink. It is not that John Daly and Martin Agronsky deserved these tributes less, but that Vincent De Paul Garrity deserved them more.

There's the story of Taft conceding the nomination to Ike, via ABC. As Vince passed it on to me, it went something like this:

Taft is staying at the Congress Hotel. Or is it the Blackstone? Vince and an engineer, fully equipped, get off at the senator's floor. They are grabbed by Secret Service men.

"Where do you think you're goin'?"

"To see the senator."

As Vince and his colleague are shoved toward the button and "down" is pressed by a hammy hand, he loudly proclaims. Though his voice carries through the corridors, the announcement is casually offered. Its import is thunderous.

Vince's conversation was always offered in the manner of a proclamation. Except during those moments when he whispered state secrets conspiratorially, hand cupped to mouth—arcane mumblings I never at any time understood.

Vince: Ya know what I mean?

Me: What?

Vince: [Slightly hurt] What I just told ya.

Me: Oh, sure.

Vince: You're my buddy.

Me: I know.

Vince: My right arm for ya.

Me: Ya don't have ta.

Vince: [Wistfully] If I only had your law diploma.

Me: It's just paper.

Vince: Not to me. [Suddenly, hand shoots toward mouth] See that guy there? Know who that is?

Me: Who?

Vince: Shh! I'll tell ya later. [index finger of right hand tugs slightly at right eyelid]

He never did tell me.

To the Secret Service men, one of whom has him by the collar: "You know who's waitin' to talk to Senator Taft on the other end? Cardinal Stritch."

The heavy hand falls away. "Stay right here."

In a moment, one of the SS men returns. A touch of apology. "Okay, go right in."

In the senator's room, whatever needs hooking up is hooked up; the telephone is beeped. The senator, stiff and formal, is ready. On the other end is John Daly of ABC. Another coup. As Vince later explains it: "John Daly's Catholic."

Consider this Vincentian tale of the same affair. He, Vincent De Paul Garrity, is experiencing some difficulty getting into the amphitheater on the night of Ike's acceptance speech. The members of the Secret Service are, for some reason, less than appreciative of Vince's stick-to-itiveness. So he does what comes naturally. He bedecks himself in the uniform of a Chicago policeman. "I was the shortest cop in the history of the force." He finds himself on the platform. Of course, Ike is in the wings, awaiting the moment.

Do you understand that moment? There is always an anticipatory ten seconds or so, when nobody is quite sure what to do. The nominee is nervous, clutching the papers in his hand, waiting. The network commentators whisper softly, reverently waiting. Millions of Americans are watching, waiting. All is sweaty pomp. Suddenly, there appears on the TV screens, coast to coast, a singularly short, squat, squinty-eyed, bespectacled policeman, leading by the arm a bewildered, baldheaded national hero—toward the ABC microphone. Of course.

Huge figures grab at the cop; he is spirited off the screens. That he is unceremoniously booted out of the hall is of small matter. A friendly member of the local constabulary spirits him back in, so he—seemingly just another face in the crowd—may taste the fruits of his existential heroism.

History may indicate that General Eisenhower, in the year

1952, made his acceptance speech, haltingly, perhaps, but muddling through, into a microphone on which are writ large the letters *ABC*. Where did Teddy White chronicle that? Do any of those pundits know what time it is?

If you think the above anecdotes are apocryphal, you and I, dear reader, must part company. True, my sole source was Vincent De Paul Garrity himself. Nor will I deny that, at times, he did engage in flights of fancy. I'd be among the doubting Thomases, too, were it not for the fact that Vince and I worked together for two memorable years.

It was a post-midnight radio program, *Sounds of the City*. It was conceived by the diabolical Red Quinlan. Only a spirit with the soul of a freebooter, gloriously so, would bracket Vincent De Paul Garrity and me. As a mutual friend of times gone by, Chet Roble, reflected: "What a quinella!"

It was a two-hour compote, free form. Our challenge was to capture the after-hours life of this city. Sometimes I worked in the studio, interviewing a writer, perhaps, or One-Arm Cholly, the Mayor of Bughouse Square, or a small-time bird of prey (usually escorted into the studio by Vince as "our wonderful lifelong buddy"). Often there were beeped phone calls to anonymous heroes and heroines: a currency exchange clerk who pressed the alarm button, thus saving his employer fifty thousand dollars.

Me: I guess you're a hero.
He: I guess I'm an ass. S'pose that button didn't work.
Me: Would you do it again?
He: Hell, no.

Most often, Vince was elsewhere: on the roof of city hall (how he got there was no business of mine); at the scene of a robbery, no more than thirty seconds after it occurred (how he got there was no business of mine; when I'd ask, the index figure of his right hand tugged ever so slightly at his right eyelid); with a night-shift bridge tender; with an ecdysiast, whom he grandly led into the studio as "the best dancer since Irene Castle." And when he called in with late news, he would offer it in truly Vincentian fashion: "Ya know who just died?" He'd name an octogenarian banker, intone a soulful eulogy, and add: "Now for some *sad* news. A small boy was hit by a truck on Ashland Av'noo . . ."

At times, music was playing. On the other end of the phone, Vince was curious.

Me: It's Mozart.
Vince: How many precincts did he carry?

Nor shall I ever forget the rainy night we wandered into the hotel where I lived as a boy. As I sat in the lobby, talking into engineer Roger Hanson's mike, nostalgic, wistful, remembering the men long gone, Vince was moist eyed. "Ah, Studs, if these walls could only talk . . ."

"Yeah, Vince . . . ? " mumbled I, gulping.

"Ah, Studs, how many votes this place could carry . . ."

And when Johnny Groth, star outfielder of the Tigers (and Chicago Latin School alumnus), was seriously beaned by a wayward pitch from Billy Pierce, it was headline news. That very night, the injured Groth called in from his hospital bed. "Everything's fine, Studs. Tell everybody I'm okay." It was thoughtful of Johnny to call, but I was bewildered. He was in the intensive care unit.

Me: Is Vince there?
Groth: Yes, he's right here.

Vince: Your old pal, Johnny Groth, wanted you to have the news first.

I had never in my life met Johnny Groth.

Vince explained it all the next day. Nobody was allowed to see the ballplayer; it was serious.

Me: How'd you get in?
Vince: They barred the door.
Me: How'd you get in, Vince?
Vince: I got a little black satchel and said I was Dr. Garrity, his family's physician.

Do you still doubt that Vincent De Paul Garrity deserved all the kudos won by the others in '52? Yeah, that was Vince. But it wasn't all of him.

One night—was it one o'clock in the morning?—Vince called in from somewhere on West Lake Street. He was phoning in a conversation with a seven-year-old black boy. I remember, word for word, how it went.

Vince: What're ya doin' on the streets this late?
Boy: Findin' bottles.
Vince: You a bottle finder?
Boy: Yeah.
Vince: What do ya want to be when you grow up?
Boy: Dunno.
Vince: A policeman?
Boy: Uh-uh.
Vince: Fireman?
Boy: Uh-uh.
Vince: You wanna be mayor?

Boy: Uh-uh.

Vince: Then what . . . ?

Boy: [Mumbling] Nothin' but a human bein'.

Vince: [Excited] Say that again.

Boy: [A bit louder] Nothin' but a human bein'.

Vince: [To me] How do ya like *that*, Studs?

I liked it fine, Vince. Yeah.

That was some time ago. Vince was some time ago. I miss him.

Frank Tuller, in Memoriam, 1975

FRANK TULLER DIED. So they say. He was an engineer at WFMT. He was the one I saw each day, behind the glass window of the control room, fooling around with all sorts of dials, buttons, and reels of tape. The birth certificate says he was forty-one years old. The hell with the birth certificate. No damn piece of paper is going to tell me how old he was. Old? Let me tell you something: He was no older than Huck Finn. I'll let you in on something else: He *was* Huck.

He was one of those rare beings in whom the young boy never died. In the great many of us, the boy is murdered all too soon and we become "responsible men," solemn, important, and dull. In Frank, the spirit of irrepressible delight was never crushed. Always, he was filled with wonder. It was as though each day he were newly born. Something terribly exciting was happening. Something good. While the others of us groused and mumbled under our breaths about one stupid thing or another, he saw the sun. And it was warming. "Gee!"

At times, one or the other of us would get so *mad* at him. "Frank, get with it, for God's sake! People are rotten!" He'd just stand in that damn doorway, freckles and all, the country boy from Kalamazoo. Playing around with the ring of a million and a half keys that dangled from his belt, janitor fashion. Or goofily mussing up his shock of red hair. "You really think so?" He'd look at you in the manner of a small boy, quizzically, with the intimation of a crooked grin. You'd furiously fumble with some of the junk piled high on your desk, hoping he'd go away. No, he'd just stand there, talking about some crazy thing that had nothing to do with what we were talking about. An encounter on his way to work. There were *always* encounters on his way to work. Or going up in the elevator. Or in the hallway. Something wondrous.

The funny thing is, his non-sequiturial anecdotes turned out to be *exactly* what we were talking about. Somebody or other was helping somebody else or other out of some jam or other. It was his way of telling you people weren't that rotten, after all. There was no stopping him. Wearily, you'd lay your head against your hand and look at him. "You should've been there, Studs. It was really funny. This old lady was hollering at this poor guy, only she wasn't mad or anything like that. It just seemed that way, you know what I mean?" You'd mumble inaudibly, get up, and head for the studio, where we had much work to do. He'd follow, his story continuing without pause. "For Chrissake, Frank, let's get the tape rolling or we'll be here all night!" "Wait," he'd say, "lemme finish. You ain't heard the best part."

My guests had arrived, but that didn't stop Frank. He included them in on his marvelous tale, italicizing it with a wink or a light jab. "Watch out for that Studs, know what I mean?" Hand cupped at mouth, a mumble, a conspirational whisper. The Swedish playwright or welfare mother or Hungarian scientist was befuddled, of course. A sudden, astonished audience. Though these guests had no idea what the hell he was talking about, they were entranced as well as mystified. One thing I know: He made them feel more at home than I ever could in a million years. You see, there were no strangers in Frank's world. No one was alien to him. He was not only full of wonder; he was wonder*ful*.

Take what happened in the elevator. Always. It never failed. You know how people are at the end of a workday, or for that matter any time, cooped in, going up, going down. Silence, the glum sort. Deadpan. Enter Frank. A light laugh is heard. The elderly secretary, the dour one, is now smiling. I have no idea what he mumbled as he gently nudged her. Neither did she. A tap on my shoulder. The whisper. "Know what I mean?" I hadn't the faintest idea what he meant. But it worked every time.

Down below is the loading platform. The underground. Nobody is allowed to park his car there. Nobody but Frank. There are hotshots all over the place. Now and then one of them tries to get cute and park his Jaguar or Toyota up against the building. It *is* very convenient. "Beat it, mister." The maintenance men and janitors, displaced Hungarians, Yugoslavs, Poles, and Appalachians, are adamant. They were impervious to a bribe of any sort when it came to this. But Frank's Volkswagen was something else. And the only thing he ever gave any of them was his presence. But that was more than enough. On days when he parked elsewhere for some reason or another, they showed their hurt. "Wassamatter, Frank? You don't like us anymore?"

If you want to call it magic, that's okay with me. But that wasn't it at all. Take that cold, dark night somewhere in the West Side ghetto. There was a meeting in the church basement of the Contract Buyers' League. Frank and I pulled up in a truck loaded with expensive and heavy recording equipment. There was a gathering of young men on the corner, quite close to us. Were they members of the Vice Lords, or what? They appeared to be glaring at us. Or was it the stuff in the truck? As I ambled into the church to see the people in charge, I heard Frank casually call out, "Hey, will you guys give me a hand?"

The tough-appearing young blacks were busy. Each was carrying something into the church. Frank was telling them where to put the stuff. He and they were giggling. They appeared to be sharing some kind of secret to which nobody else was privy. So help me, I heard one of them address him as Frank, though at no time did he give his name.

The meeting, an exhilarating one, was over. As I was talking to the chairman, I noticed some of the young men hurrying off with the equipment. They were whispering something to one another and laughing softly. As I said, it was very expensive stuff. I excused myself and shuffled after. "Hey, uh, guys . . ." It wasn't very loud. I doubt whether they heard me. But somebody did. It was Frank, who had reentered to pick up another piece.

"What's up, Studs?"

"Uh—nothin'. Nothing at all."

"Oh, I thought I heard you say something."

"No, I just—forget it."

Frank's eyes widened. As though something quite remarkable had occurred to him. He looked at me with just the hint of a funny smile. I looked away.

"Hey, Studs, you didn't think—did ya?"

"Nah, nah, nah. You kiddin'?" I was staring hard at the design behind the altar. In other days, this Baptist church had been a synagogue. The six-cornered star was hardly visible, but even if it were I'd have had a hard time making it out. Damn! Why doesn't that Frank go away? I heard a light laugh behind me.

"Oh, man, for a minute you had me goin', Studs. For a minute I thought you were scared the guys were rippin' us off. Geez!" I kicked at the chair. More violently than I had intended. I bruised my shin. Damn that Frank!

Outside, Frank was shaking hands with the street guys. They were patting him on the back, as the last piece of equipment was shoved into the truck. Frank mumbled something wholly unintelligible, at least to me, but the others thought it was terribly funny. They howled with delight. Frank nudged me. "You know what I mean?"

I think so, Frank. Knowing what you mean and have meant all along. I wish old Barry Byrne had met you. I think he'd have felt more hopeful about things. "We're caught in a treadmill we created," said Barry. "There isn't too much any human being can do to change it. If we, as St. Francis of Assisi, were of that simplicity of spirit, it might change. But that is not the way the world is, see?

"And yet, in the individual must lie the way out, because he is society. It can't be ordered. It must be achieved. This achievement is so simple. It probably will not be done. Everybody looks for miracles, wonders. We live in an age of wonders. You look for something not wonderful, for something that is simple, yet *yours*. You get tired of wonders. In the simplehearted person, finally, is the solution. A society so pervaded will make it. Not the doctrine of the announced idea. The man must listen to man himself talking."

In Frank was all that Barry was talking about. In Frank was all that Mark Twain was writing about when he created Huck Finn. In Frank was that irrepressible spirit that would not die. Let's face it; in Frank is the hope of the world and the light of life.

Frank Tuller is dead. So they say. Maybe he is. And then again, maybe he's not. True, his kind doesn't grow on trees. But if you look around hard enough and listen hard enough, who can tell? Know what I mean?

Chicago is the city where Gabby Hartnett, the popular Cubs catcher, once exchanged autographs and hugs with Al Capone. Yet it still has one of the most brutal police departments in the country. And a governor who was sent to jail, at the same time he might have been a candidate for a Nobel Peace Prize. Convicted former governor George Ryan was the first head of state with the guts to, in effect, end the death penalty. It was he who cleaned out death row. In some instances, as late as the eve of execution, thanks to DNA evidence it was discovered that inmates were wholly innocent.

There were city scandals outrageous enough to match any other in the country. There was a police commander renowned for the torturing of prisoners, retired and living on a fat pension in Florida. Chicago is after all a human city, and Janus, the two-faced god. Consider two Chicagoans who lived in two flats next to each other. They had never exchanged a word.

Chester Kolar

CHESTER KOLAR, a technician at an electronics plant. There were glory days. Once, he had conducted a program over a foreign-language radio station. He was celebrated in his community then.

"I'm cold to it, these Vietnam photos. And most of my friends, the technicians, are cold to it. The only thing is their remark: 'What do you know about that?' If you're gonna worry about that . . . and today we got so many people that are so easy to falling on this category of worrying, that's actually what makes a lot of people sick. Some people can't stand this. They shut the TV off. You heard of the guy who kicked the TV tube and took a pistol and shot into the—I mean, he was off his nut. I don't know if you ran across some of these people; they're very nervous-type people. As a matter of fact, if someone shouts, they jump. I'm cold to it.

"These people sit around this radio and TV and they listen to all these broadcasts. I think this news we're having is doing us more harm than good. I'm speaking of those that are disinterested and it's being crammed down their throats. Over the radio comes a message. Special bulletin: so many people killed. I mean, what are they trying to fire up? This poor man that's trying to get his eight hours of work done to keep his family going, pay his rent, and buy his food, which is so high today, he gets all excited about what's going to happen. What does John Q. Public know what should happen? Let's not stick our nose into something we know nothing about.

"Why should he worry about these things? We should know once a month; let's have a review of the news: what will happen and what has happened. These people are worried about something they shouldn't be worried about. They should be worried about painting their rooms and fixing something up where they could become industrious." *

* *Division Street: America* (New York: The New Press, 1993), pp. 26–27.

Stanley Cygan

STANLEY CYGAN was seeking Eden, too, when he came to Chicago in 1909, after long years of hard labor in the McKeesport steel mills. He had started at sixteen.

"The boys coming from Poland, my age, they all worked hard. My mother said the Poles were downgraded in McKeesport. 'Go to Chicago,' she told me."

Here, through all his tough work years at the rolling mills, he dreamed of books and school and finding out. "I wanted to be smart." He lost track of all the Hull-House lectures he attended, forgetting his aching muscles, listening hard.

"There was a professor lecturing on relativity." As he pronounced the word slowly, rel-a-tiv-i-ty, enunciating every syllable, there was more than awe. It was a wanting to possess the idea. "Einstein." He caressed the name. "I'd spend an hour and a half listening to the professor. But the worst of it was I didn't understand half the words he used. I never did understand relativity. There's a lot of things I don't understand. If I had more schooling I would. I want to know what is going on."

WHO'S GOT THE BALLOT?—
RED KELLY, 1975

IT WAS THE FIRST TUESDAY in November. The year, 1934. FDR had been in the White House two years. Though the will of the electorate put him there, it was the lousy aim of a nut named Zangara that kept him there. The loony drew a bead on the president, but, Miami being Miami, the bullet went wild. Anton Cermak, our sainted mayor, took it instead. "I'm glad it was me instead of you" were his reputed last words to the Hyde Park squire. (Though his grammar left something to be desired, his heart, unfortunately for him, was in the right place.) Thus Big Ed Kelly became our high monkey-monk. Thus in his choosing Little Dick Daley as heir to this palatinate, the Hibernian line of succession was established. Were it not for an errant piece of lead, a Bohemian or a Pole might well have been "the greatest Mare any city ever had." Of course, this is mere conjecture, having nothing whatsoever to do with the story. And yet . . .

November 1934. Though the goose hung low—the breadline beginning to resemble an endless, silent, gray snake dance—there was a salubrious note in the air. Flutelike. Something around the corner. Not prosperity, no. That had always been around the corner, but never made the turn. No matter how many incantations were offered by a shaman named Hoover, the snakeline was sinuously growing. (WIN, the buttony bromide of Mr. Ford, has precedents equally banal, and equally effective.) No, it was something else. There was a deep Depression, true; but an elfin air pervaded, as insouciant as Roosevelt's tilted cigarette holder. There was an unexplained gaiety that November, forty long, lopsided, cockeyed years ago.

Less than a year before, the Volstead Act had been repealed, much to the astonishment, though delight, of H. L. Mencken. The Sage of Baltimore thought it would take decades before the Temperance people would holler uncle. In less than one year after Roosevelt's inauguration, the water of life flowed legally as well as freely. "Pour some my way" replaced "Benny sent me" as the folksay of the day. Which, of course, added just the right touch—a burst of creative energy, Bacchanalian, if not Dionysian—to the polling place on Ohio Street, just off Wells. It was on other days a fire station. But on this cool November day, it was a memorable place. At least, for me. It was to be my instant school, my seminar, my arena of Revelation.

What the village of Combray was to Proust, the Forty-second Ward was to me. As the ever-lingering taste of his Aunt Melanie's madeleine touched off his memory flow, so the sensation of a harsh dram of Chapin & Gore did it for me. Oh, remembrance of things past! In my mind's eye, I see it now . . .

Red Kelly cornered me on the eve of that Election Day. (He was not related to Big Ed, though their forebears did come from that same poetic patch.) How can I describe, after forty years, one such as Red Kelly? Did he come out of some strange head of cabbage? Or some crooked alley? Or perhaps arisen out of the waves, covered with seaweed? He appeared ageless. He could pass for sixty. He could pass for twelve. His wrinkled face and puny body told us he was undoubtedly a leprechaun who had migrated to the New World during one of those frequent potato famines. Life in the big city had transformed him from a brownie under the mushroom to a child of the streets. He was a gamin, or as his kind were called years ago, a street Arab. In one manner or another, he survived. It was not politic to ask how.

"Wanna make five bucks?" Red asked of me during that unforgettable twilight.

"Sure," I replied without hesitation. Five dollars was no small potatoes in 1934.

"Okay. You be poll watcher for Mary Daley."

"Who's Mary Daley?"

Red Kelly looked at me with forbearance. "Mary Daley is the grievin' widow of Johnny Joyce."

"Who's Johnny Joyce?"

"Who *was* Johnny Joyce." Clearly, there was more here than met the eye.

"Who was Johnny Joyce?"

"Johnny Joyce," Red patiently explained to me, "was our great state senator, may he rest in peace. And Republican ward committeeman. See 'at tavern across the street?" A bony finger pointed at Friendly John's. "He owned it. Just across from where we're standin'."

We were, at the moment, standing near the alley, where many transactions of a sort took place. Where a small-time gambler named Froggy, by means of loaded dice, educated young newsboys in the truth of Horatio Alger. Where ladies of the evening met scores of the morning. Where, as the gold of the day met the blue of the night, Red Kelly persuaded me to enter Chicago politics.

"Johnny Joyce don't own the tavern now." I volunteered this information.

"Of course not." Red was fast becoming impatient with me. "He's dead."

"How did he die?" I was congenitally curious.

"You ast too many questions. You wanna make five bucks or don'tcha?"

"I wanna."

"Okay. You're poll watcher for Mary Daley."

"What's she runnin' for?"

Red Kelly sighed, weary of it all. His new recruit was slower than he had bargained for. "She's runnin' for state senator."

"Johnny Joyce's job?"

"Johnny Joyce's old job. He died four years ago, fer Chrissake! Charlie Peace is state senator."

"Charlie Peace?"

"Must ya repeat everyt'ing I tell ya? Charlie Peace is the Republican state senator, and Mary Daley don't think he's clean. So she's tossed her hat in the ring."

"She's turned Democrat?"

"No. Ed McGrady's the Democrat. She's runnin' as a independent."

"She's not gonna win." I ventured this well-considered opinion. Having been a devoted seventh-grade follower of Fighting Bob La Follette, the third-party candidate for president in 1924, I was profoundly knowledgeable in such matters.

Red Kelly took a deep breath. "Who said anything about winnin'? She's runnin' as a spoiler. Who do you think is payin' her to pay you for the five bucks?"

"Ed McGrady?"

"You ast too many questions. Mary Daley is runnin' in the name of clean politics."

"Is Ed McGrady clean?"

"You wanna make the five bucks or don'tcha?"

"I wanna make the five bucks."

"Okay."

An understanding having been reached, my mentor laid his right hand on my shoulder. "Since yer my buddy, I'll let ya in on a secret. Can you keep yer lips buttoned?" I nodded. Red cupped his left hand to his mouth. What followed was sotto voce. "Nobody knows how Johnny Joyce died. It's a mystery. Know what I mean?"

I nodded, having not the faintest idea what he meant.

"Dere are rumors makin' da rounds. They say somebody very, very close did it."

"Did what?"

"Shhhh!" He looked around nervously, much like Elisha Cook Jr. in *The Maltese Falcon*. Now that I think of it, he looked like Elisha Cook Jr. Immediately, he cupped both hands to his mouth in the manner of a megaphone and bawled out, his voice carrying halfway down the alley, "It was prob'ly an accident." To me, softly, "Accidents happen, don't they?"

"Sure." I knew he would not contradict me on that one.

"Ya know what slogan Mary's runnin' on? 'Keep the Home Fires Burnin'.'"

"I like that."

"Who don't?"

Both hands were now on my shoulders. He was Coach sending me onto the field with a play. "Ya know what ya gotta do tomorrow at the pollin' place?"

"Yeah, watch."

"You got it. You be there first thing in the mornin' and stick it out till all the ballots are counted."

"What if I see somethin' wrong goin' on?"

He studied my face. Did I detect hurt in his own? "What did I tell ya yer supposed to do?"

"Watch."

"Okay, watch. That's what yer paid five bucks to do." Suddenly he pulled away from me. His face was hard. He was no longer Elisha Cook Jr. He was Jimmy Cagney. "Hey, you ain't one of dem reformers, are ya?"

It was my turn to be hurt. "Red! Do I look like one of dem?"

"No, ya don't." He smiled knowingly. He winked. I winked back.

So it was that on Election Day 1934, I was a watcher for Mary Daley. (As far as I know, she was no kin to Himself; no more than Red was to Big Ed. That she was a Daley and he a Kelly, you may chalk up to poetic continuity and the peculiar ethnic nature of Chicago politics.) From early that day, as by the dawn's early light I saluted the Stars and Stripes, hanging outside that fire station on Ohio off Wells, until well past midnight—I watched.

There were five elderly men seated behind a long table: three clerks and two judges. They were each to receive $7.50 for their day's labor. They were chosen by the precinct captains of the two major parties. I was acquainted with two of them. They had been guests at my mother's hotel. They were bottle babies. Nor did their three colleagues appear to be friends of Mrs. Tooze of the WCTU. A carefree sort of bonhomie prevailed. And a faint whiff of sour mash.

Nothing too much was happening. There were a number of

familiar faces among the voters. That is, they had become familiar, having entered the polling place several times that day, having done their duty as Americans several times. In some instances, the *X* marked on the ballot was in the nature of a proxy vote on behalf of some dear departed, whose name was still among those registered. You could not help but be profoundly moved.

Who was to begrudge the familiar face a buck or two for each appearance? Outside, along the sidewalk, within saluting distance of the flag, the kindly precinct captain or an associate, whispering in reverence, was generous to a fault. And there were still fifty days till Christmas.

There were, as I recall, about a hundred more votes cast that day than there were on the official lists. How can this be interpreted other than as a tribute to the patriotic fervor of those citizens? What a sorry contrast today, with such voter apathy.

It was at nightfall, after the polls had closed, that things began to happen. Aside from me, the other watchers were: an earnest, pale young man who bore Republican credentials (no smile); an elderly woman who was a Democrat (a laughing Allegra); and a policeman in uniform.

The paper ballots were piled high on the long table. The counting began. A sweep was in the making for the Democrats. U.S. senator J. Hamilton Lewis was swamping his opponent, Ruth Hanna McCormick, the colonel's cousin. The night before, Red Kelly let me know that J. Ham was his buddy, that J. Ham was one of the boys. Senator Lewis was renowned not only for his oratorical flourish, but for his attire as well. From his pink whiskers, lovingly curried (he was called, by his buddies, Doctor Brush), to his pince-nez, to his diamond stickpin, to his pearl gray spats, he was a portrait in elegance. He was, indeed, one of the most expensive servants our state ever had.

He bore a remarkable resemblance to Yellow Kid Weil, that most exquisite of confidence men. It was hard to tell where one left off and the other began.

It was a shoo-in for Doctor Brush. But what about the race between Charlie Peace, Ed McGrady, and Mary Daley? J. Ham may have been Red Kelly's buddy and all that, but I was paid to watch for Ms. Daley.

It was about ten o'clock when he entered. He was the Himself of our precinct, Prince Arthur Quinn. To call him a precinct captain tells you nothing. That he was to become state representative and lots more may be of passing interest, but it tells you nothing. That he left this vale of tears quite suddenly may be tragic, but it tells you nothing. That glorious night, I remember Prince Arthur strolling in, as members of royalty have done for centuries in all monarchical societies. *He was regal.* His pink flesh, a royal baby's. His green fedora, a crown. His was not the plump of a bartender. No, he was as round as Edward VII. We were all at attention. He was Upstairs to our Downstairs.

They called him Prince Arthur because he was the son of a kingmaker. Hot Stove Jimmy Quinn. Hot Stove Jimmy was called Hot Stove Jimmy because it was around the hot stove of his haberdashery shop that many were named but few were chosen. It is said that he was among the grand viziers who selected Carter Harrison the Younger as mayor. Prince Arthur came by his title rightfully.

On entering the polling place, Prince Arthur was greeted by his subjects as crowned heads usually are. The three clerks and two judges arose from their seats. It was a matter of reflex. With a benevolent smile and an airy wave of the wrist, he bade them down. He glanced at the rest of us, nodded; we bowed ever so slightly. Ever so slightly. No curtsies, no nothing. After all, we were not subjects of the British Empire or of imperial Russia. No, by God, we were a free and independent race of Americans.

Genuflection came in the form of a greeting, an awed murmur:

"Hullo, Artie."

"H'ya, boys. How's it going?"

"Great, Artie. It's a sweep."

"That's nice." He looked toward the policeman. "Any trouble?" The officer shook his head. "Uh-uh." Again. Prince Arthur said, "That's nice."

To the five weary old men, he said, "Finish that fifth I brung downstairs?" They all smiled, abashed. Prince Arthur chuckled softly. "You guys better watch it. That's the third soldier you killed. People might think you're alcoholics." He turned toward the earnest, pale young man and smiled. No response. He was Mount Rushmore, that one. The prince slipped a package to one of the old men. "A fresh one. We're celebratin'. Take it downstairs. And one at a time, huh?"

"Thank you, Artie."

Prince Arthur Quinn, at length, seated himself on the long table, one well-shod foot touching the floor. Casually, he flipped through the pile of paper ballots. He mumbled, as to himself: "McGrady. McGrady. McGrady. Peace. McGrady. McGrady. Peace. Daley. 'Atta girl Mary. Peace. McGrady—"

"Hey! You're not supposed to do that!" We all looked up in astonishment. It was the earnest, pale young man. The world stood still. Prince Arthur's mouth hung open. I remember it even now. A tableau. The young man was pointing a trembling finger at the prince. The pink flesh of Prince Arthur was fast taking on a blushing hue. The others of us watched, transfixed.

After what seemed forever and a day, Prince Arthur murmured, ever so softly, "What'd ya say? Did I hear ya right?"

Young Galahad insisted. "You're a precinct captain. You have no right to sit on the table and finger ballots that way. That's only for the judges and clerks."

Prince Arthur looked toward the policeman, who looked toward Prince Arthur. "Frisk that guy."

The officer, in a businesslike fashion, went toward the young troublemaker, spun him around, and patted all his pockets, administering a smart slap here and there. "He's clean, Artie. Nothin' on him."

The young man, who obviously didn't know up from down, was obstinately indignant. "You can't do that to me!"

Prince Arthur shook his head sadly. His voice was gentle, mournfully so. "Throw 'im out." Which the officer did.

Prince Arthur Quinn resumed the count of the ballots, which, during this untoward interruption, had never left his hands. The young man was banging at the door. The prince told the policeman, "Ahhh, what the hell. Let 'im back in." As the young man reentered, Prince Arthur was the hurt parent lecturing the disobedient child. "Will you behave yourself?" The young man nodded. "Okay. Go downstairs and help yourself to a drink."

"I don't drink." This one was really righteous. The others of us had had a drappie or two of Chapin & Gore. The breath of Laughing Allegra was, by this time, one hundred proof.

"That's what I figured," mumbled Prince Arthur, the intimation of a pout on his baby mouth.

The ballots were being leafed through, counted, and tabulated by the three clerks, the two judges, and Prince Arthur Quinn. As the night was drawing to a close and the stack on the table was thinning out, something lovely happened; a moment I shall forever cherish. One of the judges, his glasses perilously slipping toward the end of his nose, appeared bewildered by something he had discovered on one of the ballots.

"Hey, Artie. Look at this one. I never seen this before. What'll we do with it?"

Prince Arthur held out his hand. The long pink sheet was put in it. He casually ran his finger down the ballot, and suddenly stopped. He looked up, his baby blue eyes wide with wonder. "What the hell! Communist!"

"Yeah, Artie. The guy marked it that way and wrote in 'at name. It's spoiled, ain't it?"

Artie was bemused. His usually smooth brow was furrowed. "Communist. Communist."

"Should I throw it out?"

The prince was lost in a brown study. Slowly, the crow's-feet disappeared and his face relaxed into its usual baby-fat smoothness. He smiled. It was for all the world. "Ahh, what the hell. Leave it in."

It was in that beau geste of Prince Arthur Quinn, in that gracious act of noblesse oblige, that I experienced my moment of epiphany. Let totalitarian states defy us; let dictators rave madly; let those who live in thralldom eat their livers. It matters not. We are blessed. How glorious to live in a society of free and fair elections.

The following night, at the headquarters of Mary Daley— in what had once been the meeting hall of a German turnverein—I learned another indelible lesson. We, the hardworking members of Mary Daley's watch and ward society, were to be paid off. I looked about for Red Kelly. He was, after all, my clout. I had never met the lady. She wouldn't know me from Terrible Tommy O'Connor. I had five dollars coming. No Red around and about. I saw fat ones and skinny ones,

gimps and bruisers. Highpockets and peewees. But where was
my leprechaun? I hadn't seen him since our alley transaction
on Election Eve.

Ed McGrady had won the state senatorship quite handily.
Charlie Peace was *o-u-t*. Kaput. FDR's fireside chat had seen to
it that all the Ed McGradys, from sea to shining sea, won quite
handily. Mary Daley had not drawn enough votes to alter the
result. In our precinct, though, she drew three times as many
votes as the Communist. He pulled one. Nonetheless, Ed Mc-
Grady and the boys were grateful to Mary for the goodness of
her heart.

At the headquarters—with the banner, slightly tattered but
flying proud, "Keep the Home Fires Burning"—Mary Daley
spoke eloquently. "I personally wanna thank each and every
one of you for the wonderful job ya did. We made a great
showin', no matter what anybody tells ya. What counts is we
got our feet wet and Charlie Peace was left high and dry. We
won a moral victory. 'At's as good as a real one. All right, everybody, get in line and Angie will pay you off. An' don't forget
the refreshments in the back room."

Angie, Mary Daley's campaign manager, had one arm. It
was bruited about that he was a minor member of the Boys'
Club and that, at one time or another, he had offended a major
member. The gimp seated beside me, licking an Eskimo Pie,
burbled conspiratorially, "Know how Angie lost da arm? He
had fat eyes for Louise Rolfe." Louise Rolfe! The blond alibi of
Machine Gun Jack McGurn. Madonn'! His ice cream dribbled
onto my mackinaw. "Lookit 'im. He coulda been in da
movies." Come to think of it, Angie did look a little like
Valentino. Except for that missing arm. The gimp leaned
closer. I backed away, into the shoulder of Zybysco. Or at least
a guy that size. He occupied two folding chairs. "I had a chance

to be in the movies, know dat? Wit' Lon Chaney." I was wiping melted chocolate off my pants. "Yeah, they chopped his arm off just like that. He'll know better next time, eh?" I recognized the biblical injunction, if only in paraphrase: *If thine arm offend me* . . .

I saw a thick wad of bills rolled up in Angie's one fist. The manner in which he peeled each off to pay the faithful was wondrous to behold. Though I was near the end of the line, I saw fives, tens, and even twenties handed out. At last, it was my turn. Mary Daley was checking off, Angie at her side.

"Who'd ya work with, kid?"

"Red Kelly."

Her smile vanished. Angie's one fist closed tight on the green. He roared. "Red Kelly!" Where is that miserable son of a bitch?! Where is he?"

I was stunned. "I don't know."

"Ya don't know?"

"No." I was terrified. I stared at Angie's no-arm. Would this be my fate? He may have been a minor member of the club, but I hadn't even been that. And if I offend him . . .

"The kid don't know." Mary smiled at me, beatifically. "Give 'im the fin."

Angie handed me the bill. I skipped the refreshments as I slunk out into the Clark Street night.

Only later was I to discover that Red Kelly had worked for all three candidates. He had even recruited the earnest, pale young man who had so absurdly challenged Prince Arthur Quinn. Thus, it was a second lesson I had learned that first Tuesday in November, forty years ago. Election Day 1934. Cover all your bets. You may never win, but you'll never lose. Oh, rare Red Kelly!

YA GOTTA FIGHT CITY HALL, 1973

Most of these pieces are reflections of neighborhood people—thoughts about themselves, the city—and their dreams. Our town is more celebrated for its heels than its heroes and heroines. Our heroes and heroines are unsung. They are rarely quoted. They don't make the financial page. They don't hold press conferences. They don't work for city hall (and it certainly doesn't work for them). In the words of Nelson Algren, they live behind the billboards. But they are the heart—a bruised one, more often than not—of the city.

I can think of nobody better to start things off than Florence Scala. About ten years ago she began to speak out. She and her neighbors were trying to save the place where they lived—Harrison-Halsted. It was the most polyglot of all Chicago neighborhoods. There was life; there was color; there was passion. Now there is a fortress, popularly known as the Circle Campus. There are expressways. There are complexes. There is a lot of cement. There is a lot of money. But there are hardly any people. The fight was lost. But out of it came Florence Scala. And her vision.

There was evoked during this conversation a bittersweet memory of a last walk we took down Halsted Street: Florence, my young son, and I. It was 1962. But now it is 1973, and Florence Scala is speaking:

"YOU REMEMBER THE PASTRY SHOP in Greektown?
Mrs. Poulos? The delicious sweets she gave us while we sat
there. It was her last week. Mr. Drossos joined us. He was
the principal of the Socrates School. I don't know what happened to Mrs. Poulos. Do you know what happened to Mr.
Drossos?"

*About a year or so later, I had paid him a visit, somewhere on the Far
West Side. He was much more than a year older. He was lost without his
old friends. He spoke of the diaspora. They were all bulldozed out and
went their separate ways. Gone was the Academy. He called it that: where
the old Greek intellectuals of the neighborhood sat in cafes, discussing politics, art, and life. All gone. "Nostos" was the word he used for the feeling that caught at his heart. It derived from "nostalgia" (he pronounced
it the Greek way): "When you feel a pain because you cannot return. In
Greek, anything that is nice, sweet good taste, we call "nostimo." It par-
takes of the feeling of nostos." Yes, dear friend, Florence, I thought as
her gentle voice overwhelmed me: Mr. Drossos died. Old age, someone
said. I know better.*

"The bulldozers were there. They were tearing down the
houses. Remember Dolly Belmont at the cigar store? How furious she was! Where's Mayor Daley gonna put us, in Grant Park?
And Victor Cambio of Conte di Savoia, that wonderful grocery
that had foods from everywhere. The fragrance . . . Tearing
down the buildings of Hull-House. There was a Japanese elm in
the courtyard that came up to Miss Binford's window."

*Jessie Binford had been Jane Addams's colleague and lived at Hull-
House for fifty years. Until the very day the wrecking ball blasted away
her room. She returned to Marshalltown, Iowa, to die. She was ninety but
she did not die of old age. She and Florence, those last days, became close
and dear to each other. Said Florence, "There are the little blessings that
came out of the struggle."*

"It used to blossom in the springtime. They were destroying

that tree, the wrecking crew. She asked the man whether it could be saved. No, he had a job to do and was doing it. I screamed and cried out. The old janitor, Joe, was standing there and crying to himself. Those trees were beautiful trees that had shaded the courtyard and sheltered the birds. All night the sparrows used to roost in those trees. It was something to hear, the singing of those sparrows. All that was soft and beautiful was destroyed.

"The main building of Hull-House was retained. It is so changed it looks like a Howard Johnson restaurant. I pass that building every night. The children and the students have no idea what Hull-House really looked like. Or what it was.

"There's a college campus on the site now. I call my neighborhood the Circle Campus parking lot. That's all we are for the campus and the medical center. Our streets are choked with cars. Perhaps the college performs a needed function. Yet there is nothing quite beautiful about the thing. It's walled off from the community. Jane Addams was against walls that separate people. She believed in a neighborhood with all kinds of people. She wondered if it couldn't be extended to the world. Either Jane Addams brought something to Chicago or she didn't.

"The cool cats, the tough boys, saw to it that urban renewal was working for them a hell of a lot better than it was working for us. It was a boon to the big realty boys. Their stooges did research studies over and over again for every crappy little project. They always came up with something; somehow we always lost out. One of these city planners became chairman of the Hull-House board. Almost overnight a decision was made to locate the Circle Campus there. It was the end of innocence for people in the community who thought they belonged to the city and its public servants were theirs.

"This is what the crosstown expressway battle is all about today. It would cut across twenty-two and a half miles of the city from north to south. Right now, only those living in that corridor are fighting that battle. The rest of us are on the sidelines. We've been conditioned to think of it as their problem, not ours. But we'll all be affected. The frustrations of all of us are in this struggle.

"They've raised important questions, the people of CAP [Citizens Action Program]. The phenomenal cost. The permanent tax losses to the city. The environmental factors, involving health and safety. Where will the people who live there move? It could be another diaspora, similar to the one that occurred out my way ten years ago. A respected urbanologist, Pierre de Vise, dismisses the opposition to the expressway as strictly emotional. That's arrogant. The people who live there want to be there because their roots are there. It's more than strictly emotional. If we lose our roots, what good is a city? Are we to be nomads forever?

"De Vise raises the point that blacks, who are stuck in the ghetto, must get to their jobs out in the suburbs, where so many industries have moved. He suggests car pools. That's the sort of emergency measure we used during World War II to save on gas. Are we to live forever with emergency measures? He did a good job in pointing out how segregated our city is. Wouldn't he do better fighting to desegregate the city for minority housing and in the suburbs?

"All the citizens of Chicago, not just the politicians or the highway lobby or urbanologists, should make a decision on such projects. There should be public hearings in each ward about a comprehensive plan. Haven't we had enough of piecemeal measures?

"The State Street Council and their associates are worried about downtown. They should be. At night, you can shoot a cannon and nobody will hear. There may be young black people seeing black exploitation films, but that's about it. When I was young, that's where everybody came to have a good time—downtown.

"The big money has drawn up a fantastically expensive and incredibly stupid plan for the central area. It's jazzy. But they show no interest in what's happening north of the river or west or on the South Side. The Loop cannot live without the rest of the city. Planning must be for the city as a whole, not something piecemeal.

"They envision the Loop as a garden shopping center, with two levels for pedestrians: a street and an overhead walkway. Oh, boy, can I talk about that! At the Circle Campus are walkways the students hardly use. They're not protected from the wind and the rain and Chicago's elements. I know. I've walked across them. The students use the ground level only, because it's protected by the buildings.

"The central area plan throws a few crumbs to the middle-income and working classes. They see the railroad yards south of Harrison for middle-income housing. Superblocks. Super-buildings. They will be nothing more than a jazzier kind of Robert Taylor Homes."

It sounds Orwellian. Like a fortress. Surrounded by what?

"Surrounded by us, the people on the outside. The lake on one side, the Loop, and then *us*. The plan has nothing for the people who are worried, the people who are hating, the people who are sick—all of us on the other side of the tracks."

Years ago, the people who lived "on the other side of the tracks" were "the undeserving poor who are always with us." Today it is the blue collar in the frame bungalow, the black project, the Latin in his barrio, the southern white in Uptown, and, lo! the woebegone Indian nearby. As well as the beleaguered middle middle class, who don't quite understand who thus beleaguers them.

IF YOU WERE GOD

A STREETWORKER BROUGHT ME TO a conflict going on near a public housing project about to be wrecked. A swimming pool is what the shouting was all about.

There were Puerto Ricans, African American kids of eleven or twelve, Irish, Italian, and an Asian kid or two. The stereotypes and insults were in abundance.

"What would God do in a case like this? What does he look like?" The Puerto Rican kid takes over. "If I were Italian, I'd say God is Italian, because he looks like him. If I were black, I'd say God is black. I'm Puerto Rican, I'd say God is Puerto Rican. Don't you see? You always want somebody great to feel like you, look like you—so you could feel great."

"If you were God, how would you handle this situation?"

"Are you crazy? I wouldn't want the job of God. Never. He can't do a thing about it. Give that job of God to somebody else, not me."

Part Two

NIGHTHAWKS, 1971

The reason Hopper's Nighthawks *always astonished me when I visited the Art Institute is that there was an all-night diner down below the Wells Grand Hotel and I recognized those people. The man sitting there eating by himself could be having his big meal of the day, "graveyard stew"—it is toast dunked in hot milk. He could be Sprague, from the Wells Grand, whose teeth were knocked out by the vigilantes during the 1918 general strike in Seattle.*

EACH OF US—depending on luck, circumstance, or a rainy day—may encounter a work that reveals and exhilarates. For fortunates passing through Chicago, it is Hopper's *Nighthawks*, quietly exploding on the south wall of the Art Institute. The scissor-faced customer, his seared companion, and the bone-weary counterman hold you; the slightly hunched back of the loner, whose face evades you, haunts you forever. Yet, that alone isn't what Hopper is about. It is the light that is the hero. Or is it the darkness of the street outside? One is artificial, the other natural; both are given equal weight. As Alexander Eliot observed, "The dark is less lonely." Here are all the open all-nite beaneries you have ever experienced. Here is everyman's lonesome valley.

You are offered one man's vision of America, with his profound attachment to the familiar: the city, the town, the countryside (no idyllic landscapes here, the rural past being overwhelmed by the industrial present, the captured moment of change). And it is all luminous. His was the singular American light as distinguished from, say, the Parisian light he had discovered in earlier days.

Whether it be *Room in New York* or *Hotel by a Railroad* or *Sunlight in a Cafeteria* or *Office at Night* or those old houses, the aloneness is deepened by the light. Remote from the person, it would appear—his men and women being so often in shadow and featureless—and concerned with the environment, Hopper overwhelms with a feeling for both. As his persons, in the light, sun or electric, turn away one from another, he is telling us of alienation without uttering a syllable.

The cold of the city was touched by Hopper as by no American painter, before or since. The woman, nude or half-dressed, usually near the window, was his most intimate human.

*   *   *

Hopper once said that truth in art is what's truly modern, so that "Giotto [could be] as modern as Cézanne." It certainly makes Hopper infinitely more contemporary than any Now darling you can name. Renewed wonder and humility—the artist's own phrases—are what he's all about.

On one occasion, he cited Emerson, regarding an earlier painter: "In every work of genius, we recognize our own rejected thoughts; they come back to us with a certain alienated majesty." That goes for Hopper. And all he ever wanted to do was to paint sunlight on the side of a house.

A CHRISTMAS MEMORY, 1973

WAS IT THE CHRISTMAS SEASON OF 1933 I best remember? I had reached my majority. It was a blessed year for
other reasons. The Volstead Act had been repealed. Bootleg-
ging was out. Pimping was in. Alphonse Capone, our city's
most distinguished entrepreneur, aside from Sam Insull, had
switched from the craft of alkie running to the fine and lively
art of Pandarus. His was among the first conglomerates of the
flesh. The Lexington, the Winchmere, and God knows how
many cribs in Cicero had become a home away from home for
the girl from Bloomington, Cedar Rapids, and Fond du Lac.

Small-town madonnas were, by some grotesque alchemy,
transmuted into big-town magdalenes. Quicker than a trembling, pimply faced boy could hand over a two-dollar bill. Eros
was getting a bad name. Yet, on that Christmas Eve, Virtue tri-
umphed. And the God of Love smiled benignly.

At the time, the Swede from Galesburg was chanting plain-
tively:

Nobody knows now where Chick Lorimer went
Nobody knows why she packed her trunk . . . a few old
   things

And is gone.
Gone with her little chin
Thrust ahead of her

Nobody knows where she's gone.

I know. I found out on that Christmas Eve of '33. She was a guest at my mother's hotel. Herod led her up the golden staircase. He was otherwise known as Nick Stassiosous, proprietor of Victoria No. 2, the all-night beanery. He laid five dollars across the desk and said the girl was his niece from Terre Haute. A music student, he furthered informed us. As I stared at "her soft hair blowing careless / From under a wide hat," he took the key and shut the door behind them. I had no idea he was a music teacher. Were they carols I was hearing? The bells of paradise, perhaps? My Adam's apple was bobbing wildly, as though some piece of forbidden fruit was forever stuck in my throat.

And where was John the Baptist on this holy night? He was in the lobby, holding forth, roaring, "Woe unto them who call evil good and good evil; who put darkness for light, and light for darkness; who put bitter for sweet, and sweet for bitter. Isaiah 5:20." He reached a crescendo: "Prepare, all ye sinners, prepare!" This one was otherwise known as Steve Chch, the Croatian pearl diver.* Not only was he penniless; he didn't have a vowel to his name. He was rich, though, in portents and warnings, shouting out hellfire sermons, Gideon Bible held chest high. There was room at our inn for everybody. Ours were the winking Gospels.

* A euphemism for dishwasher. This footnote is designed for post-Depression readers and those otherwise not acquainted with our city's transient life of another day.

John the Baptist was forever prophesying the world's end. Yet, his appearance was not that of your everyday nutty sidewalk Jeremiah. No glittering eye of the Ancient Mariner here. (Though he did once work in the galley of a Greek ocean liner and was fired for flinging a dish of moussaka at Aristotle Onassis's uncle; such was the nature of his religious fervor.) No long black coat or long gray beard. His were the baggy pants of a burlesque comic and glasses thicker than George Zucco's. (This last, you remember, was movies' mad scientist.) The fact is he was as cockeyed as Ben Turpin and as myopic as a mole.

Regularly, his fever high, he posted special delivery letters to Franklin D. Roosevelt, Mahatma Gandhi, Albert Einstein, Benito Mussolini, and Babe Ruth (who, he figured, also had clout). As well as to Ramsay MacDonald, Britain's prime minister. As well as to Alphonse Capone, who sponsored the biggest breadline in town. (Al, the Good Samaritan, was often applauded by the multitudes as he and his Roman battalion took their box seats at Cubs Park.) For good measure, he sent equally urgent communiqués to Herbert Hoover, Henry Ford, and David Lloyd George. He was aware that Pontius Pilate was dead; no letter for him. I am certain his earnings as a pearl diver (five bucks a week plus free blue-plate specials) went in large part toward the purchase of stamps. They were impressively thick envelopes. We were, all of us, in awe.

As fate would have it, John the Baptist was sweating his life away in the kitchen of Victoria No. 2. Nick Stassiosous was his boss; a singularly abusive and exploitive one.

John the Baptist and I had tasted little of life's forbidden, and thus delightful, fruits. He neither drank nor smoked nor, the other guests were certain, had ever known a woman. I had touched nothing stronger than Dr Pepper. Within one hour, during this remarkable Eve (Eve?), our two lives were considerably altered.

As Herod and his niece from Terre Haute were engaged in a music lesson upstairs, the chimes from the Tribune Tower sounded "God Rest Ye, Merry Gentlemen," "Adeste Fidelis," "Good King Wenceslas," and "Go Tell It on the Mountain." Though the effect on the pinochle players in the lobby was somewhat euphoric, their thirst was unslaked. Some son of a bitch had killed the last pint. They were still cold, cold sober. Distemper was in the air. Sprague, the journeyman carpenter, and Ed Duerr, the railroad fireman, were passing words. While the Prince of Peace was a-borning. Some celebration. Go tell it on whose mountain?

Enter Prince Arthur Quinn, holding high a fifth of Chapin & Gore. Placing the treasure carefully on the table, he proclaimed, "Merry Christmas, boys." It was now official. Prince Arthur, son of Hot Stove Jimmy Quinn, was our precinct captain. It was his annual show of appreciation. Aside from Election Day, when Chapin & Gore had the persuasive powers of ward committeemen. Though our guests numbered fifty, they counted for one hundred at the polling place.

Beatifically, he smiled my way. I was, this year, eligible to vote. Poor old Cermak was gone by way of a goofy assassin's bullet and ever remembered for his martyred mumble to FDR, "I'm glad it was me instead of you." (Though his English teacher would have flunked him, he is immortal and she is dust.) Anyway, there was still an *X* or two or three to be marked beside the Gaelic names of Big Ed Kelly, Dorsey Crowe, and Botchie Connors.

The smell of sour mash pervaded the lobby and all spirits were buoyed. All except one: John the Baptist. He cried Damnation and predicted Apocalypse. "Woe unto them who are mighty and drink wine; and men of strength to mix strong drink." (On occasion, he was suspected of being in league with Mrs. Tooze of the WCTU.) Prince Arthur Quinn, his fedora a Kelly green and his face a beet red, grumbled, "Who da fuck is dis nut? T'row 'im out." The other guests merely smiled. There were times past when they seriously discussed throwing him out the window. It was only a two-story drop. But propinquity has its way. Though, in the beginning, they had come to jeer, they remained, if not to pray, at least to nod and murmur, "Amen."

The bottle was passed around. Eventually, it came my way. I hesitated. The men chuckled softly, nodding encouragement. All except John the Baptist. He howled. "No, boy. As the fire devoureth the stubble and the flame consumeth the chaff, so this root shall be as rottenness and their blossom shall go up as dust because they have cast away the law of the Lord of Hosts. Isaiah 5:24." The words poured forth torrentially. Though I was uncertain as to their meaning, I had a hunch they bode no good.

Prince Arthur was indignant. "Dis guy's a fuckin' fanatic. I'll nail 'im to a cross. Scarin' da kid dat way." To me, Prince Arthur beamed. "Go ahead, kid; drink up. It'll put hair on your chest." Really, I wasn't *that* glabrous. As I studied the label on the bottle, I knew a moment of decision was at hand. John the Baptist was jabbing at the air, Gideon Bible held tight in his fist. Prince Arthur was moaning, "Will ya take a drink fer Chrissake!" That did it. For Christ's sake. Never had I heard the Savior's name invoked so appropriately. On such a night as this, the God of Bliss, et cetera and et cetera.

I put the bottle to my lips. "No-o-o-o!" The wail of the pearl diver was stifled by the command of the precinct captain. "Shut up, you dirty Bolshevik!" I swallowed. My throat was on fire. I coughed. Spittle came. So did tears. I took a deep breath and once more I swallowed. Was my tongue blistered by the devil's brew as I passed the bottle to the next one? I had turned away from John the Baptist. Prince Arthur chortled. "'Atta kid. Dere goes yer cherry. Stick wit' me, kid, and I'll take ya to da Winch or da Lex. Or even Cicero. Real poontang, kid. You'll be a man before yer mudder." In the eyes of John the Baptist, I saw a thousand hells.

I followed his look. At the door were two of them: Herod and Chick Lorimer. "Artie! What da hell are ya doin' here?" The restaurateur was in an ebullient mood. "Steve, fer Chrissake!" The precinct captain was of equally blithe spirit now. A kindred soul at last. He whistled softly through his teeth as he observed the girl. "Hey, ya doin' aw right fer a Greek, huh? Huh?" A long drawn out, "Yeah-h-h." Herod touched the girl's sleeve. "Oh, yeahhh. She's a good friend o' mine." Turning to her: "What's yer name again, baby?" Chick Lorimer stared at the lobby's linoleum. Again, my Adam's apple was misbehaving. And a sense of some vague humiliation I couldn't get a fix on.

In the exuberance of the exchange, neither of them noticed John the Baptist. In his eyes I now saw a *million* hells. "Pi-i-mp!" It was a howl. No, it was more a cry of the banshee wholly at discord with the nearby chimes' "Silent Night."

"Wha-a-a-a?" Herod stared, mouth agape.

"You pimp! You bully! You fat, no-good Babylonian! Woe unto them who call evil good and good evil; who put darkness for light, and light for darkness; who put bitter for sweet, and sweet for bitter. Isaiah 5:20." God, did Isaiah say all that? John the Baptist, it appeared, really had a fix on this one.

Prince Arthur took a step away, toward Herod. "Dis guy's a real loony. Could be dangerous."

Herod extended his thumb in the direction of his tormentor. "He's my goddam dishwasher! Da crazy Serbian!"

"I'm *Croatian*, you fool! You ignorant Macedonian! Do you write to Mahatma Gandhi? No! Do you write to President Roosevelt? No! To Albert Einstein. Henry Ford? No, you do not! Do you know the Holy Bible?" He thumped at the book. "No! You know nothing. Pimp! Pimp! Pimp!"

Herod, recovering his composure, held forth his pinky, the diamond of its ring shimmering in the light. "Yer fired! Did ya hear what I said? Fired! Come in my restaurant, I'll t'row you out on yer ass! Yer t'rough!"

"And you're damned!"

It happened so suddenly. The Gideon Bible was hurled across the lobby. It struck Nick Stassiosous below his right eye. A direct hit. His hands flew to his face. "I'm blinded!" A long agonizing wail. "Da bastard blinded me!"

Chick Lorimer casually drew his hands away from his face. She hardly glanced at him. An angry red welt, with intimations of blue-black, was quickly puffing up. "You'll have a beaut of a shiner is all. You'll live." "It ain't yer eye, ya whore! Jeez, it hurts. I need a doctor!" With a whimper, he turned and hurried down the golden staircase.

Prince Arthur Quinn was edging toward the doorway. He cast a wary glance at the lunatic. This was a serious matter. The green fedora disappeared as a faint murmur was heard: "I'm gettin' da cops. Dis guy's dangerous."

John the Baptist was transfixed. A mist formed on his glasses. Mist or no mist, cockeyed or myopic, he saw Chick Lorimer. He saw her stoop down and pick up the book. She walked across the lobby and handed it to him. She grinned. "Good throw. Cubs could use you." John the Baptist was mute. She laughed lightly. Again, I had trouble with my Adam's apple. She was straightening out the collar of his torn jacket. "Know the Book of Luke?" He nodded. "Cat got your tongue?" He shook his head. "Okay, then you can read me the story of Mary and Joseph and no room at the inn and all that, right?" He nodded. She took him by the hand and led him out of the lobby.

At the doorway, she turned toward me. "Sonny." Sonny! Christ almighty, she was no more than nineteen herself. Sonny! Damn! Damn! Damn! Damn! "The Greek ran off with the key. You got a skeleton, ain'tcha?" I nodded. A lot of good that nod did me.

John the Baptist was at the window of her room, feverishly leafing through the book. Muttering to himself: "Woe is me, for I am undone, because I am a man of unclean lips; for mine eyes have seen the King, the Lord of hosts." He didn't seem too unhappy about it, though. At the door, she asked softly, "How far to Cicero?" I told her. The door clicked shut. In the lobby, I joined the others. There were still several ounces of Chapin & Gore left in the bottle. This time, it went down easier. While the journey to Bethlehem was being recounted upstairs, the Trib Tower chimes were sounding. "Hark! The Herald Angels Sing."

UPTOWN

Uptown attracted us. In 1977 my wife and I moved here. At the time, it was a way station for many lost Appalachians and Ozarkians, for the mountain people. Today SUVs occupy the space of three Appalachian owned flivvers. Today it is gentrified compared to what it once was, years ago. At that time, Native Americans hid in doorways with muscatel in paper bags, and the mountain people looked for voices. During my first day there, I wandered toward the bus, past a schoolyard full of little kids, black, Asian, white, all nationalities, first-, second-, and third-world.

Suffer the Little Children, 1980

THE FOOL'S PARADISE was a schoolyard in Uptown.

The Fool's a fool any way you look at it. Consider the manner in which he salutes the little kids each morning, Monday through Friday.

It's 8:45, always 8:45, give or take a minute on his Timex, as he passes by. It is a primary school on the corner of a tree-lined street in Uptown, precisely at the spot where the haves and have-nots meet. Patiently, the little cubs, calves, and colts await the morning bell. The more energetic chase one another in and out of the grounds. Their parents, working people, have just driven off in jalopies or wearily walked away. The Fool approaches from the east.

They are from five to ten years of age, the Fool guesses, but they appear to be younger, smaller, as though lately out of swaddling clothes. They are of every shade, color, and society: Korean, Appalachian, East Indian, African, Thai, Japanese, Afro-American, Filipino, Colombian, Vietnamese, and a smattering of "ethnics." The Fool delights in the picture. They exude the sweetness and innocence of a UNICEF Christmas card. They are, in his mind's eye, child images of U Thant, Wole Soyinka, Emiliano Zapata, Rabindranath Tagore, Emilio Aguinaldo, Woody Guthrie, Pelé, and Chief Tecumseh. It is a small-change Eden as evoked by, say, Rousseau. One world forever.

Though he is bundled up against the cold, his red muffler is dashingly unfurled. "Good morrow, Robin Goodfellow," he calls out to the assemblage. On another occasion: "What news on the Rialto, Tybalt?" Then, again: "Good morning, dear hearts and gentle people." And always, he salutes them, his hand held toward the heavens.

During the first week, all is well. The kids stare at the wayfaring stranger, eyes wide. A few giggle. A black boy, no bigger than a bar of soap, has a khaki book sack on his back, a World War II hand-me-down. On it, clearly printed with a felt-tip marker: "George Johnson." Naturally, the Fool calls out, "How now, George Johnson?" The small boy spins around like a top. He looks up, his eyes all wonderment. He whispers, "How you know my name?"

"I know everything," the Fool sings out. The little girls, doing a circle dance, stop and stare. The Fool runs toward his bus.

He is not certain when he first senses a change in his matutinal acquaintances. Casually, it makes itself felt. As they see him approaching from some fifty yards away, they jump up and down, run around in circles, and point small darts of fingers in his direction. They are delighted, the Fool surmises.

As he passes by, greeting them with his usual ebullience, one, a small Thai child, takes a swipe at his behind. It is hardly felt, a light slap. The Fool is astonished. Though he holds up his hands as in surrender, his voice admonishes, "Uh-uh, no, no." From the other side, another slight bump. It is a mite of a Guatemalan child, a startlingly lovely little girl of six or so. As the Fool runs for the bus, he hears delighted giggles, squeals, and shouts. He has hardly felt anything, other than a small fall from grace.

Still, he offers morning salutations, after his own fashion. On one occasion, George Johnson, solemnly awaiting him, calls to the Fool, "Now, listen heah."

The Fool shuffles over, a reluctant schoolboy. "What?"

"Whatchu mean what you say ev'y day?"

"Oh," explains the Fool, "it's the way I say 'Good morning.' Or 'How are you?' 'How's it goin'?' 'Have a nice day.' Know what I mean? Friendly. Nothin' bad."

George Johnson scratches his head, looking up, studying the Fool's face. He turns away. The Fool runs for his bus.

The following day is bitter cold. Most of the kids are inside the school's hallway. A crossing guard, a red sash across his front, stalks toward the Fool, no nonsense. "You talk 'at way again, I'll whip you' ass." He's a Korean kid, nine years old at most. He tips the beam at seventy pounds, tops.

The Fool is astonished. The crossing guard turns away and strolls toward his companions across the street. The Fool's voice is unexpectedly hard: *"What did you say?"* His voice carries across the way. He cannot stop, though something tells him he's acting the fool even for the Fool. "Are you tryin' to be a tough guy in front of your friends?"

The small boy with the red sash looks surprised. The Fool runs for his bus. His outburst was something he himself hadn't anticipated. His fall from grace was, this time, less insignificant than before.

On a subsequent morning, a father from the Orient, his face furrowed from days unto days in the hard sun, is standing by his small child. The Fool, having offered the usual orotund salutation to one and all, smiles at the man. The man does not smile back. A Latino father and an Appalachian mother are also standing by. The Fool offers them his sunniest. They're not certain how to respond. They turn away. The Fool runs for his bus.

On this latest day, the children of the UNICEF card are waiting for him. He approaches. The little Vietnamese sliver and the ever-so-small Japanese kid are jumping up and down, chanting in ragged unison, "The crazy man! The crazy man!

The crazy man!" The small Filipino, the tiny Colombian, and the Tennessee tot appear more bored than sullen. George Johnson shakes his head and turns away.

As the Fool waits for his bus, he sees the blubbery old man of rheumy eyes and slight drool, ragged cap comically atop his head, a guest of the nearby halfway house. The Fool nods toward him and smiles. The man—is he Schubert's wretched organ grinder?—shuffles on. The Fool boards the bus for the last lap of his daily winter journey.

As I said: The Fool's a fool, as any fool can plainly see.

A Family Bar, 1979

SUNDAY MORNING COMING DOWN BOULEVARD: Call the street Argyle if you're so inclined, free country. Walk the strip between Sheridan and Kenmore any day, especially on Sunday, and you'll get the idea. A mother lode for Diane Arbus, were Diane Arbus still around catching our strangeness. It is our street, not "theirs." It may be a Riverview funnyhouse mirror, but it's our mirror. There is only they; there is only us. If you have any doubt, ask the Fool . . .

See. See how that raggedy kid, small, delighted Latino, call him Tico, see how he runs, darts, leaps with such agility between the U-Haul and the '67 Chevy. Hear. Hear the Paducah beauty, twenty-three going on fifty, calling out to nobody in particular. Observe. Observe. The inscrutable Oriental (Why is he so wistful?) peering through the window of his Ma-and-Pa grocery while Mama-san busies herself at the counter. The American Dream. Seoul was never like this. Or was it? Listen. Listen to the two black dandies say something funny to the lean brown girl embracing the lamppost. She can't stop laughing. Fun*neee!*

Look. Look at these three others making it down the street the hard way. The girl (Can she be more than eighteen?), Himalayan, bearing mountains of flesh, waddles on. Her face, lifted upright by mounds of chins, is a baby doll's, a *Playboy* Playmate's. She is laughing, too. Indeed, she is radiant. The companion, strutting at her left, a chocolate cadaver, Artis Gilmore in height, is gesticulating excitedly. Dig. Dig, he's making a joke. The third of these merrymakers is twisting, twitching, and Morris dancing along, though laboriously. He is palsied, cerebrally so. The hollow sound erupting tells us that he is enjoying the joke, too. Immensely. Oh, I love you, Junie Moon.

Stumbling out of Foremost Liquors, a fifth of J & B in a brown paper bag, the drunk Fool shuffles into *the* tavern. There are other such oases in these parts, any number of such places for people to get in out of the rain, especially when there is no rain at all. But this one has something going for it. Something *spess-ial*, the Welsh would say. Something edgy. Call it je ne sais quoi. The Fool has multiple choices, but he knows—don't ask him how he knows—that this is his dear-hearts-and-gentle-people place. *Entrez-vous.*

"Take This Job and Shove It." Loud and clear out of the jukebox. It's Johnny Paycheck's way of saying hello. Again and again and again. The barmaid is Ollie, hard-pretty; a miracle out of the Scriptures had she been soft-pretty after so many hard days' nights. Bad teeth. She's been shoving quarters into the machine, quarters left as a tip by the drunk Fool. Paycheck's her boy, again and again and again. Does the Fool sense that it's her way of saying shove it?

The drunk Fool, who lives in a house on a tree-lined street— close by, yet five planets away—is on his fourth boilermaker. It does seem silly, what with a good enough fifth of J & B in a brown bag at his elbow, patched, of course. His neighbor, slouched low on the adjacent stool, a weary black, age indeterminate, has a brown paper bag at his elbow, too. A quart of muscatel. You pays your money and takes your choice.

"She likes that song," the drunk Fool, who catches on quick, mumbles at his musky friend. The other shakes his head, looks at the wine while it's red, and chuckles softly as though it's a private joke between himself and his brown paper bag. He's the only black in the place. The others are Kentucky,

Tennessee, West Virginia people. Bad teeth. They're busy with one another talking Appalachian talk. A randy joke or two. A job lost, another found and lost. Tomorrow Monday Morning Coming Up, a day at the day-labor exchange. A woman who has run off, a man wearing horns. Harsh laughter. Then, soft: home. Home, that's what they're talking about most. Where they were, not where they are. They don't know where the hell they're at. Neither does the drunk Fool. His neighbor may know, but he ain't talking; that's between himself and the brown paper bag.

"I like that song," the Fool, stiff as an Appalachian recruit in basic training, says to the fifth of Early Times that's minding its own business on the back shelf.

"You better," says Ollie. "Your quarters." She refills the shot glass.

"Hey, she's pretty good," says the Fool. He grins a foolish grin at his neighbor.

"All *right*," laughs the other.

"Take this job and shove it," Johnny Paycheck defiantly growls, again and again and again.

Ollie has other fish to fry. At the street end of the bar, she nudges a seated skeleton. Something is passed about Kentucky. There is a short laugh. What the Fool hears isn't that funny, but what the hell, he joins in, too. There's nothing like getting in good with your new neighbors.

Ollie freshens his beer.

"Kentucky, huh?" He squints at her. He can do little else; his eyelids weigh heavily.

"'At's me all over," she says.

"Ever been to Whitesburg?"

The drunk Fool had been there a few months before, looking in at Tom Gish. Tom runs *The Mountain Eagle*, a local newspaper. He had returned to his hometown, realizing the journalist's dream of being a small-town editor. Among his own people. They kicked the bejeepers out of him, his own people did. Tom had written something about strip mining laying waste to the land. Tom is still bleeding. Whitesburg.

"Sure I been to Whitesburg," says Ollie. "My brother's a jailer. 'At's how I kept *outta* jail."

The Fool laughs appreciatively. He shoves two more quarters at her.

"Put 'em in the box," she says. He stumbles off the stool and does as requested. He presses B-7 four times. "Take this job and shove it." Anything to win Ollie's approval. After all, her brother's a keeper.

He points at his shot glass. Ollie pours something into it. He tugs at his pants pocket, hears the sound of ripping cloth, and comes up with two badly wrinkled bills. He slaps them on the counter.

"May I buy you one?" he says to his neighbor.

The musky man sighs, looks at the Fool, smiles, nods. "Gotcha covered."

Ollie pours out some red wine.

"How about you? Would you care for one?"

"Why not?" says Ollie, as she goes for the white.

"Miners are havin' a rough time," he says out of the blue. It's not really out of the blue; the strike's been going on for some time and the TV is full of it, telling the story in a half-assed way.

"They never had it so good," says Ollie.

The Fool shuts his eyes tight. His head is throbbing, intimations of a hangover bearing down. It is slowly dawning on him that Ollie's a fink. He's a romantic and somehow can't see the hardworking Cumberland barmaid as the mine operators' darling. Yet Ollie is indubitably a fink. And down at the other end of the bar, are they all finks, too? The whole world is finky when you're out of love. His neighbor stares into his muscatel. He shoulda stood in bed, the Fool.

"ERA women is pigs!" It is a loud *pronunciamiento* from the shadowy end of the bar. He had been aware of vague mumblings in that precinct, but hadn't noticed the patrons there. A couple of couples had been occupying space and, after a fashion, spooning. But now their presence is definitely felt.

"A man, if he's half a man, wears the pants in the family, and any woman who thinks different's a pig an' oughta be horse-whipped." The Fool shields his eyes as he searches out the voice, a no-fooling-around contralto. She is an extra-large blonde, bearing a startling resemblance to *The Muppet Show*'s Miss Piggy. Her consort is a sad, silent horse. Clearly, he's not accustomed to much talk, not in present company.

"Why do you say that?" The Fool, indubitably drunk, doesn't really know when to quit. His voice is low, mellow, as though hawking Gallo wines on TV. He has assumed his sincere, persuasive tone.

" 'Cause 'at's what they are—pigs—and oughta be horse-whipped."

"Why do you say that?" He is Mastroianni now, the smiling, silly Marcello of *La Dolce Vita*'s last reel.

" 'Cause they're pigs an' oughta be horsewhipped."

This is getting nowhere. He slides off the stool and moves toward the shadows.

"*You're* a woman," he says.

"*All* woman." It's a challenge more than a declaration.

"Well, then," says the Fool, indubitably a fool, "don't you like yourself?" Oh, boy.

"Hey." The other woman, larger than our Phyllis Schlafly and even more blond, disentangles herself from a bespectacled daddy, whose eyes are out of focus. "That's my stepdaughter. Watch yer language."

"Oh," he says, sinking deeper into the slough, "we're merely having a discussion."

He fumbles out another quarter, finds his way to the jukebox, and presses down hard on B-7. Twice. He needs Johnny Paycheck. Back at the old stand, he finds Ollie waiting for him. She is not smiling.

"Sir."

"Yes, ma'am."

"This is a family bar."

"Oh, I know."

"We can't have that."

"We were just having a friendly discussion."

"Sir, this is a family bar."

"May I have another beer, please?"

Ollie flips open a Meisterbräu and carefully pours it into his glass.

Ollie calls out cheerily to the others at the far end that she's knocking off for an hour. Her relief is a mustache and long legs in a cowboy hat. He's laughing about something or other. "OK," he announces, "Johnny Cash is here."

The fool is hearing Johnny Paycheck and wonders, Why not Johnny Cash? He's out of quarters.

"Where you from?" asks the Fool.

"Tennessee. *T* for Texas, *T* for Tennessee." This one's full of good cheer. The Fool feels better. Maybe those guys down there are not finks, after all. Maybe they're ex-miners, blacklisted or black-lunged. Maybe. And maybe he's J. Paul Getty.

He gets a good grip on his brown paper bag and slowly, carefully, as though walking a tightrope, moves toward the door.

On the Magnificent Mile, somewhere between Kenmore and Sheridan, invigorated by the Sunday air, he finds himself galumphing alongside Junie Moon and her two companions. Junie, all four hundred pounds of her girlishness, is laughing, still laughing. Artis Gilmore is gesticulating excitedly. Their buddy, twisting, twitching, and Morris dancing along, is letting go with a hollow noise, clearly enjoying the joke. The Fool, his brown paper bag clasped to his pouch, like a kangaroo's baby, is smiling. Now they are four.

Aaron Barkham

"ONE TIME THEY HAULED A MULE OUT." They fired the guy that got that mule killed. They told him a mule's worth more'n a man. They had to pay fifty dollars for a mule, but a man could be got for nothin'. He never had worked another day since. Blackballed for costin' 'em that money.

"An old woman, about sixty years, she come down from Canyon Creek. One time she was makin' a speech near a railroad track. She was standin' on a box. The strikebreakers shot her off with a shotgun. . . .

"The county sheriff had a hundred strikebreakers. They were called deputies. The company paid him ten cents a ton on all the coal carried down the river, to keep the union out. . . .

"They brought the army in. The country was under martial law, stayed till about thirty-one. What strikes me is the soldiers along the company road, dispersin' people. When people'd gather together, they couldn't talk. Two guys could, but three couldn't.

"About that time, a bunch of strikebreakers come in with shotguns and ax handles. Tried to break up union meetings. The UMW deteriorated and went back to almost no existence. It didn't particularly get full strength till about 1949. And it don't much today in West Virginia. So most people ganged up and formed the Ku Klux Klan.

"In my life, I've found people won't take anything. If things get real bad again, I'm afraid there'd be some millionaires made paupers because they'd take their money. They'd take it the rough way. The people are gonna take care of their families, if they'd have to shoot somebody else. And you can't blame 'em for that. You think I wouldn't take what you got if you had a million dollars and I had to protect my family? I sure would. I'd take your money, one way or the other. Some people don't have courage enough to fight for what they have comin'. Until 1934, more than half the people of Logan County were scabbin'. Gives you an idea how they don't know . . ." *

Barkham, black lungs and all, came to Uptown, too. Obviously, he patronized another kind of bar in Uptown.

* *Hard Times: An Oral History of the Great Depression* (New York: The New Press, 2000), pp. 204, 206.

A Voice from a "Hey, You" Neighborhood, 1973

Peggy Terry is usually described as "a poor white." She is certainly that; she is also Peggy Terry, an individual. She lives in Uptown, where so many Appalachian and Ozarkian émigrés are crowded together in rickety furnished flats. They are often charged by the week. Like poor blacks, they provide bonanzas for absentee landlords. Like poor blacks, they were, once upon a time, considered faceless. Though the psychic depression is deep, so is the anger.

"HILLBILLIES ARE UP HERE for a few years and they get their guts kicked out and they realize their white skin doesn't mean what they always thought it meant."

She reflects on her personal experiences, on race and on life in the big city.

"Almost any black says what I would say, were I better educated and had more words at my command. I've found that being poor white trash really means I learned about my own history in starting to read black history. Influences on my life—church, schools, the air you breathe—tend to make you feel you're not really worthwhile. While you're deeply racist, you don't think about yourself. You still have a terrible burden of guilt. The way I came to know myself was reading black history. It's a long story how I came to do that. The first thing that I read was *Before the Mayflower* by Lerone Bennett, and it just blew my mind. So many things I didn't know. When I realized that the beautiful history of black people had been kept completely from me, I became interested in myself."

Many black people can't live where they want. Can you?

"No, because I don't have the money. This is just as bad a wall as the color of one's skin. This is one of the funny jokes, in the country: There are no poor whites. Nobody talks about us. The middle class is deathly afraid of us. They're more afraid of us than they are of blacks."

Why, Peggy?

"Because we look like them, but we don't think like them. Our way of life is more like Puerto Ricans, like poor blacks, like any other poor people. Nobody wants to admit this. What they say to us in various ways is 'You're white and you could make it if you really wanted to.' It isn't true, because this economic system will not absorb all the people who need jobs, and if all the whites in this country were educated, who would they get to go in the Klan? Who would pick cotton and do all those hard and terrible jobs?

"A lot of this is being automated now, but it wasn't when I was growing up. My folks were sharecroppers. They were a little bit of everything to stay alive. We traveled back and forth from Kentucky and Oklahoma. I married a young boy who was from Alabama and went there to live when I was fifteen. It's the same trap. But it takes you a long time to figure it out, and this is what they don't want you to figure out. They don't want you to figure out that you have anything in common with Spanish-speaking people or black people or any other kind of poor people. You're white and they drill that into you, and this is supposed to make up for your hungry belly. When you figure all this out, you're goddamned angry that you've been stupid for so long. It took me forty years to figure this out. And I'm ashamed. I think of a song Bob Dylan wrote: of the poor white in the caboose of the train. He talks of how the sheriffs and mayors, the cops, all get paid for the kinds of dirty work that they do for the rich. And don't make no mistake about it: they do it for the rich; they don't do it for the poor."

She reflects on the double standard we follow in judging people.

"Talk about the city, how people are separated from each other. How we judge only by appearance. I remember an article I read in *Psychology Today*. They did an experiment. They had a well-dressed man with an expensive briefcase and all the trappings of the upper middle class stand on a street corner and go across the street against the light. People followed him. Then they had a man who was dressed very poorly, old, dirty, and he walked against the light. No one followed him. The people were very angry at him. They made nasty remarks about him not obeying the laws. When I read that article it frightened me because I realized how far we have gone for images. Both of these men came from the same background, but it was the way they looked. They wouldn't follow the man who was poorly dressed and was a little dirty, but the man who looked 'respectable' they followed. This is frightening and I see it's just part of the city.

"In Alabama I picked cotton, chopped, hoed. In the next field over there were black people but they had absolutely nothing to do with me. They were doing the same kind of work for the same pay; everything was exactly the same except they were niggers and I was white. It made all the difference in the world. Didn't really, of course. When we went to the valley of Texas, we worked as migrant workers. I worked mainly with people from Mexico who came across the border, some legally, some illegally—whatever illegal is. I hate these lines, international lines, state lines. I hope to see the day when all those lines are done away with. They don't mean anything, not really, not when people know each other. It's another way they have of separating us.

"We were picking grapefruit, oranges, limes, lemons, and we sat down to eat our lunch, which consisted of a jug of luke-warm water and biscuits made early in the morning. And I was sitting there eating, and I saw this little Mexican boy reach over to a bush and pick a berry, and I thought, well, with biscuits something should liven it up, just biscuits and water. So, I reached over to a bush and picked one. Well, my God, it was like liquid fire; it was just horrible. And he started laughing he was rolling on the ground, just laughing. Then he realized I was in pain and he went to the grapefruit tree and picked one off and tore it apart with his hands and gave it to me and told me to suck on the grapefruit. And my mouth was burned so badly that I had water blisters, like a fever sore blister, and he thought that was so funny. So we got in this conversation, about Anglos and food. I didn't know what an Anglo was. He thought it was so funny that Anglos couldn't eat the berries and he could, and this made him very important. You see, he felt very good about that and I felt very put down. We got to be good friends and it helped a great deal toward my understanding. I was still leery of the grown people, but I began to like the children."

At one point in the conversation Peggy Terry was talking about sense of personal worth and the regulations and the sense of living in a huge city and wondering how much of it you own.

"When you figure who you are, suddenly you're very proud and you know those streets belong to you, and you say, Damn appearance! I pay taxes; these streets were built with my money. No matter how poor you are. In fact, the poorer you are, the more taxes you pay."

She has thoughts concerning urban renewal and the mayor's Model Cities program.

"I once saw a band marching down State Street celebrating

Model Cities. I thought of it as a death dirge. It shows how little communication there is. What is Model Cities? It is Mayor Daley's plan to get rid of poor people. Where the Circle Campus sits today was a beautiful neighborhood, and a very beautiful and strong woman, Florence Scala, fought a battle there to try and stop that. She and the neighborhood lost. What they're trying to do is get poor people out of Chicago. I think that they suddenly discovered that we can control the cities. They've awakened to this. The way they're doing urban renewal in our neighborhood—we call it 'poor people removal.'

"They're not doing it like they did in other neighborhoods. Then they went in with bulldozers and there was ways you could fight that. You could put sugar in the tanks of the bulldozers, like people fight the strip mines in Appalachia. You could lay down in front of them; there were various things that were done and could have been done but weren't."

You sound like Muley Graves trying to fight the Caterpillar in Grapes of Wrath *when the homes were tractored out.*

"It's the same. It's all part of the same. But in our neighborhood they're burning the place down at night. Winos come to us because we've helped them. They come to us and they tell us who paid them to set fire to a certain building. We run one of the free clinics in Chicago, the Young Patriots Clinic. They come to us and they tell us that they set fire to buildings. They burned one of our children, who came to the clinic on Saturday. Saturdays are set aside for children, and they burned one of our children to death. How can you fight this? You wake up in the middle of the night and your building is on fire, and all you can do is flee. You live in absolute constant terror. Not only of the police, but of fire, of your children getting strung out on dope. A ghetto is a ghetto, and color has nothing to do with it.

"They don't talk very much about a white ghetto. I haven't met ten people who would admit knowing, and they probably don't know, of a white ghetto. Until just the last three years, I think the estimate was seventy-five thousand poor southern whites in Uptown. It's known as a port of entry for poor southern whites, but nobody talks about it. When we try to raise money we run into this: 'You're white, and you can make it.'

"We went to a church. The minister invited us. I went with two black women. The black women could say anything they wanted to those people, to explain the plight of poor people in general. The more the black women put them down, the more they loved it. But the minute I opened my mouth, they started putting me down. They didn't want to hear it from a white. I lost my temper and I said, 'You are afraid of the wrong people. I can go to a beauty shop, get my hair done, put on a nice dress, a hat, white gloves, and I can come out here and burn you down. I'm not saying I'm going to—I don't believe in that kind of thing—but I'm saying I could. You're so uptight about black people and afraid of them that you hand money to them. You're more racist than I am, much, much more. You sit out here and you go to Selma. Well, I came from the Selma.' They were mad at me because when Selma happened they said, 'Are you going to Selma?' And I said, 'Why should I go to Selma? I know Selma and I'm going to stay and fight in Chicago.' Well, Chicago isn't anything like Alabama! I said, 'Well, Brother Malcolm said the Mason-Dixon Line begins at the Canadian border.'

"This is our turf. And if we call the United States our turf, we should talk about Sitting Bull; talk about Custer, who died for our sins."

We hear and read a great deal about violence in the streets of the city.

"I'd say hunger is as violent a thing as possible for there to be. I remember a speech I made at one of the universities. The women in the audience kept saying, 'Why do kids in your neighborhood throw bricks through store windows?' The only answer I had for them was 'Have you ever been hungry?' Hunger is a very violent thing. If you've ever been hungry and had cramps from it, you know how violent it is."

She has strong feelings on the double standard of justice. She once told me: "As far as the authorities are concerned, you live in a middle class, a 'sir' neighborhood. I live in a 'hey, you' neighborhood."

"Everything I've learned came out of experience. A motorcycle in our neighborhood, on the corner of Sunnyside and Clifton, caught fire, and someone called the fire department. So, they came and put out the fire, and a kid in the neighborhood took one of the firemen's hats. They called the cops. All at once there were at least fifty police cars there, paddy wagons, all kinds of cops, plainclothes cops, uniformed cops, and they were running through buildings with their guns out in their hands, rushing in and out of people's apartments, opening the door if it wasn't locked, and walking in. Everybody was angry, because here is violence committed against people in the ghetto. The firemen got alarmed at so many policemen running around with guns in their hands, so they took a bicycle, a brand-new bicycle that one of the kids was on, because they definitely knew who had taken the hat. They put the bicycle on the fire truck and said, "All right, we're going to settle it. We'll keep the bicycle until we get the fireman's hat back.' Everyone thought that was fair, fair enough. So then everyone got involved in finding the fireman's hat, which really wasn't very hard to find. That settled that question apparently. But then they wouldn't give the bike back. They put kids—they were under twelve years old—into a squad car and they took off. This isn't fair. If you get the hat back, you give the bicycle back, and that's the end of it. But that isn't the way it turns out. It never turns out that way in a 'hey, you' neighborhood. The firemen, they put a young hillbilly friend of mine into the paddy wagon. And we said, 'Man, it ain't never gonna happen.' We started rocking the paddy wagon back and forth. We said 'Let him out; you're not leaving with him.' So they kept yelling 'Hey, you' at us. 'Hey, YYou!' 'Hey, YYYou!' So I walked up to them and I said, 'I'm not "Hey, you"! I'm Peggy Terry and that's Thomas Maleer in the paddy wagon and this is Nancy Maleer. And you're going to let him out before you get out of here.' I said, 'Do you call the people in Winnetka "Hey, you"? You call them "Sir." All poor people live in a 'hey, you' neighborhood. They have no names. It isn't just black people who have no names; it's poor whites also. Poor whites have become the invisible people. Blacks, through their own efforts, have made themselves very visible.

"I think of the countryside, where there's stripping going on, ruining mountains that it took Mother Nature millions of years to produce, spoiling the water, creeks, with the drinking water, and the fish; the acid from the runoff causing the creeks to be so bad that the fish actually will jump out on the banks. The conditions that we've talked about in the cities, not just Chicago, but all cities I've been in—the same thing is going on. Expressways are splitting people away from each other, alienating people. This is part of the 'divide and conquer.' The only hope I see—and I don't know if I can hope because I know they won't do it—is for the politicians to realize that we, the people, are the boss. They are *our* employees. We pay them. They are not the boss. By us sitting back for so long and not saying anything, they have taken power that belongs to the people. And the only way that any change is going to come about is for the people to get that power back.

"That's by *organizing*. I'd like to do that gently, because I truly loved and respected the Reverend Martin Luther King. I truly believed in his philosophy. But I don't believe they're going to let us do it like that. I think his death proves they're not going to let us do it like that. I don't want violence because I know who gets the worst end of it. We do. So, when they say that people want violence they're telling a damn lie, because you know who gets the violence: we do. I say, all power to the people, and that means people who are for human beings instead of buildings that say no, no, and schools that tell you you're an ignorant hillbilly, you're a nigger, you're a spic. We need schools that tell us to love life and above all love yourself. Because you can't love anybody else if you hate yourself. I think that's where racism comes from—hating yourself. You hate yourself so desperately that you grab onto something else to hate.

"Better times must come, but they can only come if we become aware of our inalienable rights as human beings. And fight for them. I hope these changes will come easy, but I doubt it. How do you say it? 'Take it easy, but take it.' "

I first heard the phrase "Take it easy, but take it" used by Woody Guthrie in the thirties. He told me it is an old piece of American folksay.

Part Three

E. Y. "YIP" HARBURG, 1978

One of America's original contributions to the world of art—you might say the world of entertainment, but more than entertainment—is musical theater, musical comedy.

One of the most deft of lyricists, but more than that, one of the most nimble witted—and lyrics often, almost always, were the point, something called residue—is Yip Harburg, E. Y. Harburg. You know of him, of course, mostly from "Brother, Can You Spare a Dime?" that bitter anthem of the Depression days, and the one from The Wizard of Oz, *of course, "Over the Rainbow." But those remarkable musicals* Finian's Rainbow *as well as* Bloomer Girl—*it's remarkable to me how they are so contemporary now, even more than when they were written. It seems to me that Yip Harburg was prescient as well as gifted at the time, and is now as well.*

Of his two books, one is available now, At This Point in Rhyme. *It's a matter of verse that brings back memories of those glorious days of verse writing with bite and wit. He will be reading some and I will be reading some; we'll hear some of his songs as well, but more than that, we'll hear what is the hallmark of a good lyricist.*

[The program opens with "Brother, Can You Spare a Dime?"]

AND THE PREVAILING GREETING at that time on every block that you passed was some poor guy coming up and saying, "Can you spare a dime?" Or "Can you spare a dime for a cup of coffee?" Now it would be about two dollars. At that time you could have gotten a double boiler and made your own coffee for a long time to come. But a dime did the trick. It was a cup of coffee and probably more, a bun.

All that "Brother, can you spare a dime?" finally hit you on every block and every street. And I thought that would be a wonderful title if I could only work it out by telling people through the song: It isn't just a man asking for a dime, saying I'm having hard luck. This is a man who says, "I built the railroads. I built that tower. I fought your wars. I was the kid with the drum. I was the guy in khaki. Why the hell should I be standing in line now? Why? What happened to all this wealth that I've created?" And I think that's what made the song live. . . . Of course, together with idea and conception and meaningfulness, a song must also have poetry; it must have the phrase that rings a bell, and that makes an impact so that it's lyrical and it isn't just prose.

And there, again, with the difference between what kids are saying now or what the young songwriters are doing now . . . I mean, it's instant writing; it's instant lyrics. They've had absolutely no foundation for it. They don't read; they don't have the background of years and years of training in classics and so on that goes into the process of writing poetry, as it would if you were a scientist. [He sighs.] Anyhow . . .

I think with that sigh right there . . . Yip is my guest here. This was a comment made by Yip Harburg when I was working on Hard Times. *I was visiting his apartment in New York about ten years ago. It's funny . . . Here you are now. We heard the chorus of* "Brother, Can You Spare *a Dime?" and then your comments. There are about three or four aspects involved. First the idea—we'll come to the young in a moment—that song was not a beggar's song.*

It was trying to expound, really, a social theory, that theory that our whole system of capitalism and free enterprise is based on a rather illogical and unscientific groundwork: that we each exploit each other, we each get as much out of the wealth of the world that our ruthlessness, and our chutzpah, and ability to step over others, gives us permission to enjoy. And most people who don't have that kind of power are left penniless, even though they do most of the producing.

Writing is life. Writing should be social awareness. And one thing that I deplore about the writing today is that instead of social awareness, it's social complaint; it's self-pity; it's bewailing the fact that things are bad, rather than exposing what's bad about them.

I was brought up at a time when we all had a background of history, and political science, and we knew that the world was constructed on certain lines that had to be reformed. And there was a great reform movement on. I mean, the movement during Roosevelt's time was formidable. We knew what we were after. We knew that we could have Social Security, which we didn't have. We knew that we could have Medicaid for the poor. We knew we could have unemployment insurance. We fought for it.

Not simply is it a matter of no substance in the songs, but the style, too. In your case, style and substance are interrelated, are they not? You could tell it's a Cole Porter song by the lyric. You could tell it's a Larry Hart song by the lyric, or an Ira Gershwin song. That is so, isn't it? You wrote "Brother, Can You Spare a Dime?" thinking as you do, and from the standpoint of this guy, this ex–World War I vet, who is now broke and out of things. If Cole Porter had done it, he'd have done it very deftly, of course, but his would have been the guy who's being asked for the dime, wouldn't it?

That's right. Well, Cole Porter belonged to a so-called smart set. He was born into great inheritances, in fact, four inheritances. He had a chateau in Venice, he had one in France, and he was living a different kind of life, and it was a very interesting kind of life. It was the kind of life we all aspired to. It was the kind of life where "I Get a Kick Out of You." . . . It was a champagne-bubble feeling in the air.

But it was so deft and so good. You and he—I think he'd have been the man who was being asked for the dime, and it would have been quite a marvelous song, I'm sure.

Right, and I'm sure he would have given the fellow a half a dollar.

Yeah, given him a half a buck! That's right. So that was his hallmark as, you know, "You're the tops, you're the Coliseum," is his. An example of yours, from that marvelous musical Finian's. *I'll ask you what you had in mind in* Finian's *and what comes out on the stage, too. "When the Idle Poor Become the Idle Rich." This is witty, it's funny, of course, the turn of a phrase; at the same time, what a comment. Why don't we hear part of this.*

This is what I am missing, Studs, in today's writing, and what I deplore, and why I will always be against it. I have no communication with it. Because when you lose humor, you're in disaster area. Show me a Hitler and I'll show you no humor. Show me a fascist state and there is no humor. Show me a democratic state ... We were noted for our Mark Twains, our Franklin Roosevelts, or Lincolns. All the great guys who had humor and gave us a sense of humor. Now, a song like "When the Idle Poor Become the Idle Rich" is profound. In fact it took Shaw, Bernard Shaw, a whole play, *Pygmalion*, to make the same point. Where he took a flower girl from the street and had a bet with Higgins that he could, with a little money, educate this girl and give her an accent so that she would not be distinguishable from anybody at Buckingham Palace. In other words, when the idle poor become the idle rich, you take on the same coloration as the rich and the cultured.

I'm thinking also about the phrase "and every relative will be a Rockefellerative."

Now we're getting into the technique of using profound political ideas in an entertaining and titillating way. And this is another thing I miss in today's lyric writing. I don't find the playful, the adroit, the ingenious use of phrase. So that people can laugh and think at the same time, and be left with meaning. And not be clobbered over the head, you know, with sledgehammer phrases. Because people run from polemics but they don't run from laughter.

You once told me something on this very point, the fact you don't like to hit something on the button. . . . There's a subtlety, and it's that that provides the—

That's always the most subtle way of getting an idea across. The subtle way is through what Churchill called "the soft underbelly of the soul," you see. And naturally, I mean, that kind of a subliminal and subtle thing doesn't arouse people, doesn't make them angry. It makes them listen, it makes them laugh, and it makes them swallow the gilded and sugared pill.

You know, one of your hallmarks is the use of the same word, the same word assuming a different meaning. A classic would be from Finian's Rainbow: *the leprechaun, Og, suddenly realizes he's like Cherubino in* The Marriage of Figaro. *Hey, he's got that feeling for that girl—girls. And here, "When I'm Not Near the Girl I Love." If ever there were a classic case of using one word in fifty different ways . . . "When I'm not facing the face I fancy, I fancy the face I face."*

Well, this is the art of songwriting, of taking a great idea and expanding it, but expanding it with surprise and twinkle, so that the audience is waiting to see, well, now, how is he gonna top this? How is he gonna make this point again? But you keep topping it, and topping it, and topping it. So the reason they're titillated is because they love the play on words; they're fascinated with it. And what they are absorbing is also an identification with the terror of becoming mortal.

You remember, this song was written for a leprechaun who was becoming mortal and began having the sex feeling, the sex urge. That's a terrifying thing for a growing person. It's one of the hardships of becoming mortal, of feeling naturally that it's a beautiful and lovely thing, sex, and that his nature tells him so. But his society and his church tell him otherwise, say it's immoral; it's indecent. And the conflict that the poor human being who is growing up is in, if it's stated in human terms, becomes a very laughable thing. And if we can laugh at the idea, we will learn how to cope with it.

In other words, whatever follies we have, whatever problems we have, if we don't feel bitter about them, and get mad and argue about them, but see them as follies and know how to laugh at them, the solution will come quicker and more peacefully. And this applies to almost everything in life, whether it's war, whether it's the conference table right now going on between Russia and America. Imagine if we had Mark Twain on this side and if they had Bernard Shaw on their side how fast there would be peace in this world, through humor. But we haven't.

And that, of course, being what you're talking about. On this subject, you're the lyricist, of course understanding the human heart, the frailties, as well as the strengths of this sad species, and yet this wonderful . . .

There was a man, Clifford Durr, whom you've heard of; you know his wife, Virginia Durr, fought way back for equity for all. Clifford Durr was FCC commissioner under Roosevelt, and he said, during the Selma–Montgomery March—Cliff was watching the scene; he was a participant, too—he said, "You know, this human species, this race, man; man created Auschwitz, yet he wrote 'Ode on a Grecian Urn.' Man committed the most awful atrocities, yet he charts the stars. Man has done horrible things to his fellow, yet he dies for a faith." And yet, just as the psalmist says, he's all. So both are in us, and you're saying, with that humor, to probe the frailties, at the same that which makes the human human. If I can be Harburgian for a moment, using your phrase, that which makes the human human.

Yes, but to become human is very inhuman most of the time.

Another aspect, and yet related, of Yip Harburg's giftedness, is his rhymes. We're talking about what is the nature of rhyme in verse, in contrast to lyric for a song. At This Point in Rhyme. He'll be reading from that. And the other—perhaps you can ask for it and maybe they can reissue that—Rhymes for the Irreverent. So the subject of verse and you. And on this very subject of the human heart and human frailties.

You hold in your hand At This Point in Rhyme. *Why not try a few of them, we'll talk about them, and I'll try a few from your other book,* Rhymes for the Irreverent.

All right. Well, of course, you know that I'm always fascinated with satire, with making points that I like to laugh out of existence; for example, our attitude toward money, and how we worship it. Here's a poem called "Heavenly Vaults."

> Where banks all look like temples,
> And temples look like banks.
> Where does one count his blessings?
> Where does one offer thanks?
> You sense the holy places
> By the faces in the ranks,
> The bankrupt in the temples,
> The worshipful in banks.

Here's my little tirade against the songs I hear today, and it's called "Music on the Rocks."

> Hail the songs, the latest rages,
> Dripping from guitar and pen,
> Are destined for the ages,
> Like, you know, I mean, from five to ten.

I've got to ask you something, Yip, that suddenly occurred to me. As you're reading these rhymes you've written, can they—writing verse and writing lyric—can they be put to music? Would they be difficult to put to music?

Yes. They could be put to music by the kind of music you have today, that is three chords and—I can make up any song that you hear on the spur of the moment, instant music. To do what they call folk music, I can take any one of these things and do it. But I couldn't do what Arlen or Gershwin or Porter did with music, I mean, to write a melody with ingenious metric involvements, and to fit words to them. You can take any one of these songs like the one I just read.

But that wouldn't be it, though; that would not be it.

It wouldn't be it. I can do this. [Sings in mock folk style] Oh, where banks all look like temples / And temples look like banks / Where does one count his blessings? / Oh, where does one offer thanks? I can do that with any song.

Lyric writing, with the music of Harold Arlen or Burton Lane, now that's something else, isn't it? Now we come to a fusion of two forms.

But I would have to get a tune like [Sings] Da-di-da-da-di / Dum-da-di-dum-da-di-dum / Da-di-dum-da-dum . . .

Oh, I love that.

That's a powerful, beautiful song. Or you take a thing like "Over the Rainbow," which Harold wrote. "Over the Rainbow," when you consider it, it's a theme for a symphony. Listen to this: [Sings] Bum-bum-bum-da-da-da-dum / Bum-da-da-dum . . . You can write a symphony around that, but you can't write a symphony around the folk song.

No. There, too, in "Over the Rainbow," the care, the jeweler's eye here. The care . . . The word "over"; you had to work for that, didn't you? You had a certain reason.

That's right, because we had to work for sound and for the emotion of the tune. For example, given a tune, which was written first, like [He sings] da-di-da-da-di-da . . . I couldn't use consonants. I couldn't say, "Say, bud." It wouldn't sing. I had to use open vowels. And look, [Sings] Somewhere *over* the rainbow . . . The *o* comes right underneath. And comes right into the thing, and that was an important part of the writing. So on top of the playfulness of words, on top of the meaning and the poetry, the sound had an importance in it. Today you don't have to worry about that at all; there is no songwriting.

You're also talking about you and your colleagues and that whole background, and the reading, the verse of Gilbert to the music of Sullivan. But also the French writers of verse, and for that matter the Greeks and the Latins, the Romans. You really had—

Yes, we were well versed in all the French forms, the ballad, the triolet, the rondo, the villanelle, the sonnet. And these were highly disciplined. You never were permitted to use an oracular rhyme, or a tonal rhyme like home and tone. There is no rhyming today, and there's no poetry today.

Do you think it's because there is a lack of continuity? That there is no sense—we're told many of the young lack a sense of history. I'm talking about the pop song—

Let's say lack of education. I don't know what the youngsters are learning in school today. I think they're learning how to photograph; they're learning how to cook; they're learning how to put wires together to make a radio set. But the humanities are out. Nobody knows who Longfellow was anymore. I asked some kids about, you know, "The Village Blacksmith." They don't even know that.

Let's continue with more of the verse. Oh, I know, the difficulty of writing a lyric for a song as against verse. Dorothy Parker, who was so marvelous with her verse—

She was great, impeccable.

Could not do it; could not do lyrics for a song.

Well, to make the transition from verse writing to songwriting is like a leap from Peter's foot to Satan's knee, or Satan's foot to Peter's knee. It's an altogether different medium. Verse writing is an intellectual pursuit. You sit at home with a book, you are quiet, you absorb the thought, you chuckle to yourself. A song done in the theater is an emotional explosion. At the end of it you expect applause. You've got to move an audience, not only with the words, but with the emphasis on the music.

So there's both. Whereas verse could be for reading and for offering, reciting, the lyric of a song is theatrical. It is very, very oral, audio.

Right. That's why we call it act one, act two. You act things out. When you act things, you're dramatizing, to have drama, song, give you that extra dimension that plain conversation does not give you. It's the same as novel writing and histrionic writing, dialogue writing for the stage. They're two different things. One has to have movement, emotion, drama, force, explosion. The other has to have intellectual perception, peace, absorption, in a quiet way. And that's why for every thousand novel writers and prose writers, there's one playwright, all right.

Shaw did both, of course; he could do both.

Shaw was a master of both. But not only that; he was not only a master of prose and the stage, but he was a master of political science; he was a master of what the world was about. He knew the theory of evolution, the Darwinian theory. He knew Freud. In other words, he was a total man. And to be a good writer, even a lyric writer, you must be a total man. You must know you're living in a world of Darwin, and Freud, and Shaw, and Einstein. If you don't know that, and if you don't combine all these things in an entertaining way in what you do, then you're meaningless; then you're only getting a hit record and making a million dollars.

You're what Lillian Hellman called "a kid of the moment."

That's right; that's right.

But you are a kid of many, many moments, sir. Yip Harburg. More of that verse. I'll take a whack at the earlier book, too. While you're looking for a verse, this is from an earlier book that I hope is available. There are three brief ones here. I'll read "Agnostic," "Atheist," and "Realist." "Agnostic":

> No matter how much I probe and prod,
> I cannot quite believe in God.

But, oh, I hope to God that he,
Unswervingly believes in me.

"Atheist":

Poems are made by fools like me,
But only God can make a tree.
And only God who makes the tree,
Also makes the fools like me.
But only fools like me, you see,
Can make a God who makes a tree.

And here goes "Realist":

For what we are about to receive, oh, Lord, 'tis thee we
thank.
Said the cannibal, as he cut a slice off the missionary's
shank.

The realist in me.

What have you from At This Point in Rhyme?

Well, here's a couple I seem to like. This is called "Fail
Safe."

It's a hundred billion dollars,
Every year at your expense,
For the Pentagon to gadget up,
Our national defense.
But it's comforting to know,
That in the up and coming war,

We'll be dying far more safely
Than we ever died before.

That's almost Shavian, too. Yet it's yours, so it's Harburgian, though; that's the irony. Just connecting that, a postscript to that one is one of yours here, "Fish and Fashion."

When the nuclear dust
Has extinguished their betters,
Will the turtle surviving
Wear people neck sweaters?

That's a fashion note.

This one is called "The Enemy List," of which I happened to be a victim once.

Lives of great men all remind us,
Greatness takes no easy way.
All the heroes of tomorrow,
Are the heretics of today.
Socrates and Galileo,
John Brown, Thoreau, Christ and Debs,
Heard the night cry "Down with traitors!"
And the dawn shout "Up the Rebs!"
Nothing ever seems to bust them,
Gallows, crosses, prison bars.
Though we try to readjust them,
There they are among the stars.
Lives of great men all remind us,
We can write our names on high.

And departing, leave behind us,
Thumbprints in the FBI.

Oh, yeah. That's, I would say, quite contemporary. You wrote that a year or so—a couple of years ago. There again, that's the old story, isn't it? There, in your seemingly lighthearted way, that's the old truth, isn't it? Those that call the shots at an early time are called traitors—

And years later they're called patriots. Yeah. That happened to a fellow named Tom Paine, remember? Galileo.

Here's one, on this very point. You open up with the question of Pontius Pilate. The question: What is truth? And here are your four lines.

The truth is so top secret,
It only stands to reason,
That anyone exposing it,
Is culpable of treason.

I have one. I have some people who are my favorite poison ivies, if you'll forgive me. And this is called "A Saint He Ain't." It's a person I have to listen to every time I turn the radio on, once in a while, by mistake.

Good St. Paul and Vincent Peale,
Are men of wholly different steel,
Yet both of holy calling.
St. Paul is most appealing,
And Peale is most appalling.

[Chuckles] Here's one. It's about critics. This is Shaw—you're quoting Shaw at the beginning.

"The professional critic is a frustrated writer"—GBS. Here's Harburg.

> When the critic, with all his frustrations,
> Is but phosphate and lime under earth,
> When this victim of fertilization,
> Can no more thwart the process of birth.
> Will some frail little daisy he sires,
> Now proclaim him expressed and fulfilled,
> And release all his hostile desires,
> From his fellows who fashion and build?
> Will the tunes and rhymes he so humbles,
> Still annoy him there under the ground?
> Where his critical cranium crumbles,
> While the songs still survive all around.

[Chuckles] Shaw would have liked that very much.

Yes. He influenced me a great deal, this kind of thinking. Here's one I like, a little quick one called "Of Thee I Sing, Babel."

> Build thee more stately mansions, little man,
> More grandioso, more gargantuan.
> But as the towers rise, and derricks roar,
> Remember there was once a dinosaur.

You know, there's a marvelous writer of nature, Hal Borland, who died recently. This verse of yours reminded me of Hal Borland's articles he wrote so often. He said: What has made man feel so arrogant that he thinks that his species won't go if he fools around too often? Other species

*have gone. He speaks of the dinosaur. He's certain that other species once
ran the world or inhabited the world, but they went, the time went, it was
over. And he says, well, if man behaves the way he does now, why don't
they think their time won't be over, too? And that's the point you made
right there.*

There's no doubt about it. From all my reading, from all my
thinking, and don't forget, I've reached an age now where I
can claim a little wisdom.

You are eighty-two, but who would believe it?

And I think that the world is an experiment. That the way a
man in a laboratory experiments with a test tube, the world is
an experiment for something on the outside, for nature. Nature wants to survive. Nature wants to have birth, creation,
growth. And it is constantly trying to find a species that will
live in harmony with its laws and all its elements. And she is
trying very hard to get that superman, the man that will live in
conjunction with nature, with all its elements. So that he won't
be neurotic. So that he will be at peace. So that he can enjoy the
beauty of all that life offers us. And so far, she has tried many
species. She has tried the albatross, and the albatross went out
of business. She has tried the dinosaur; the dinosaur went out
of business. As soon as they get too big for themselves, and
too powerful, something happens to the species. In fact, nature has tried hundreds and hundreds of species. Man is nothing more than another species of nature, which so far has
shown the greatest acumen for survival. But he is not beyond
all the others; he is not any greater than any of these other
species. And nature has no use for a guest that is not a good
guest in its logistics.

Not a courteous guest.

Right. If we can't be decent human beings and have respect for one another, and know the laws of nature, and the laws of mankind, nature's got no use for us and will wipe us out as easily as she did any of the insects.

I'm thinking At This Point in Rhyme really wittily, funnily, nimbly says all this with humor. One more from that, and then I've got to ask you about Bloomer Girl.

Well, now here is a poem, I think, in which I offer, "The Far Out Generation," in respect to what we're saying.

> The freak out,
> The flop out,
> The psyche out,
> The drop out,
> The black out,
> The fall out,
> The conk out,
> The cop out,
> The wipe out,
> The sweat out,
> The strike out,
> The sell out,
> Are warning the world,
> We may all get the hell out.

But then, as you say that, you also are saying, you speak always of the beauty. I'm thinking of that song from Finian's, "Look to the Rain-

bow." By the way, we haven't talked about Bloomer Girl. Bloomer
Girl *dealt with the suffragists, Seneca Falls, and abolitionists all at the
same time. If ever there were a contemporary musical . . . When was*
Bloomer Girl *written?*

Nineteen forty-four.

So that's thirty-four years ago. Can it be that long ago?

That's right.

*If ever there were a woman's movement musical . . . Now, you called the
shots then. That could run for years, it seems to me. If* MS *magazine
could sponsor a month of that, and now could sponsor a year of it.*

Well, I'm hoping that somebody will revive it again because it's
so apropos now. It's everything that the people working for the
ERA are saying.

*You know, just as everything is related, and I think . . . you speak of the
whole man—you're a whole man, all around. In* Bloomer Girl, *just as
you were saying a moment ago about the human species and the need for a
whole man, your artistry reflects that. Because in* Bloomer Girl *is a song
the slave sings—Dooley Wilson, "the runaway slave." It's about when
the world was an onion, the eagle and me. And you describe in a way—
you remember how those lines go again?*

Yes. We showed that the women's movement was part of an
indivisible fight for equality. Equality cannot be divided. If
there's no equality for the black man, there is no equality for

anybody, because if you can do that to one minority, you can do it to all. And the women knew that, and so they kept an underground railway in 1860, and they helped the runaway slaves to get across the border. So one of the songs in *Bloomer Girl* was "The Eagle and Me," which went . . . I wish I had some music to keep me on pitch. [He recites]

> What makes the gopher leave its hole
> Trembling with fear and fright?
> Maybe the gopher's got a soul
> Wanting to see the light.
> That's it, oh, yes, oh, yes, that's it.
> The Scripture has it writ,
> Bet your life that's it.
> Nobody likes hole,
> Nobody likes chain.
> Don't the good Lord, all around you
> Make it plain?
> [Sings]
> River it like to flow,
> Eagle it like to fly,
> Eagle it like to feel its wings,
> Against the sky.
> Possum it like to run,
> Ivy it like to climb,
> Bird in a tree and bumblebee,
> Want freedom in autumn or summertime.
> Ever since that day,
> When the world was an onion,
> 'Twas natural for the spirit to soar,
> And play the way the Lord wanted it.
> Free as the sun is free,

That's how it's gotta be.
Whatever is right for bumblebee, and river, and eagle
Is right for me.
We gotta be free,
The eagle and me.

A GATHERING OF SURVIVORS, 1971–72

FRAN ANSLEY, 21: My mother had a really big family . . . she was one of seven kids. And she brought me up, not on fairy tales, but on stories about what she and her family used to do, and that meant the Depression, and other stuff, too. So they feel almost like fairy tales to me, because she used to tell me bedtime stories about that kind of thing.

TOM YODER: My mother has a fantastic story, in my opinion, of growing up in the Depression in a small town in central Illinois. And, I don't know, from what she says, and I don't think she tries to glamorize it . . . these were times that were really tough. And it just seems absolutely . . . it's almost, in a black humorous sense, funny to me that, to realize that, you know, a hundred miles from Chicago, about forty years ago, my mother's older brothers, whom I know well now, were out with little rifles hunting for food to live on. And if they didn't find it, there were truly some hungry stomachs. And this is just . . . this is just too much as far as I'm concerned. I don't think that my generation can really fully comprehend exactly what all this means.

PAM: It's weird, because my mom is very much ashamed of the hard times in the Depression. But my aunt and uncle are very different; they're very—they're almost proud of it, and I think a lot of that is because they made it, and they got a lot of money. So they say to me . . . they talk about lazy people, and I know my parents sit there and think: Well, does that mean I'm lazy, you know, and that kind of jazz. And yet, they know they've really worked their hearts out. And I think, thinking back on that, and on my parents' feelings, and on finding out what happened, had a lot to do with my feeling like you gotta have money to make it. And my mom had the habit of having little piles of money stashed away around the house, and we thought that was really weird.

TAD, 20: It's something that's been filtered through my parents. I don't know much about it and I think that they don't mind my not knowing much about it; they'd rather sort of control this one source of information. Sort of like, I don't know, the high priests and you can't approach the altar too closely or you'll be struck dead. Because they weren't so much aware of the Depression at the time, but since then, this Purple Heart in their background has become such a justification for their present affluence that, you know . . . that if we got the idea that they didn't have it so bad, well then that would be that one less sort of psychological control they'd have over us.

CHRISTINE: For my father, I know, he talks about having gone through the Depression meant that he needed things for security, because he always felt that since like there was a big black hole out there somewhere you might fall into. And he defends himself to me a lot of times by saying, "I need these things around me, 'cause if I don't have them, that might happen again." At the same time, I know for some people it meant that they found out that you're still human even if you don't have money, and what the hell.

TOM BAIRD, 21: My father talks about it didactically, you know, and tries to draw little lessons from it, and he has anecdotes which come up every time the Depression comes up. It's sort of this heroic past for them.

STEVE, 21: So many times, people—people like us, young people—are told that idealism is fine for youth, but that there's a point one reaches when he must face up to the practicalities, the realities of existence. I think that lesson was learned during the Depression, at least to my parents that what actually happened to America was that they were forced at a point, at a period of time, to give up their idealism; forced to face up to the hard realities of making a buck and staying alive, surviving.

MARSHALL, 13: You know, I was thinking of one other issue. We talked about the value of the dollar being one difference. The other is the word "fear." America's always had a lot of fear: xenophobia, anticommunism, something or other, Red Scare after World War II. Fear, fear, fear, fear, fear. Fear, I think, is the thing that people learned in the Depression.

FRAN ANSLEY: The things that they teach you about the Depression in school are quite different from how it is. You knew that for some reason, society didn't get along so well during those years, you know. And then you found out that everybody worked very hard, and so everything somehow just got better. You never hear about any struggles that went on. A lot of young people feel angry about that. Wanting to protect you from . . . from your own history in a way.

[strains of "Brother, Can You Spare a Dime?" playing]

JIM SHERIDAN: These fellas that come with their families, and by themselves, some of them with their wives, they came mostly by boxcar! Can you imagine women and children riding boxcars? Well, this is actually what happened.

Well, many of the bonus marchers took their families with them.

JIM SHERIDAN: They took their family because after all, many of these bonus marchers had been evicted from their flats or their houses because they hadn't the rent to pay. Probably they owed the landlord three or fourth months' rent, maybe sometimes more. And some of them were evicted, and some of them just left, and left their furniture behind them. Sometimes there'd be maybe fifty or sixty people in a boxcar. That many.

We had leased a place in Virginia. It was a very hot day, and I noticed that in this jungle there was a man, a very tall man, about six feet tall. . . . He had a woman with him who was his wife, and several children, and an infant. The infant I don't think was a year old yet. And we invited them over to have something to eat with us, and they refused. Well, I could see that the baby . . . the baby was crying from hunger. Finally, I— me and some others—went down to bum the center of town, and I figured probably that they didn't have any bottle to feed the baby with, or any milk. And I remember going into a drugstore and seeing the druggist and bumming a baby bottle with a nipple. Now, can you imagine a guy bumming a baby bottle and a nipple? Then I went and bummed the milk.

When I got back to the jungle camp it was kind of dark. I addressed myself to the man's wife, and I told her here was a baby bottle and here was some milk. We had even warmed up the milk. But she looked at the husband, and the husband said he didn't want it. And what could I do about it but just feel blue that . . . The pride of this fella fascinated me, but here he was subjecting his wife and his children to unnecessary hardships because of his extreme pride. And going through the tunnel, the baby died, probably one of the unreported tragedies of that bonus march.

And when we got to Washington, there were quite a few ex-servicemen there before us. There was no arrangement for housing, and most of the men that had their wives and children were living in what they called Hoovervilles at the time, across the Potomac River. And they had set up housing there made out of cardboard and tin of all kinds. Most other contingents—it was along Pennsylvania Avenue; they were tearing down a lot of buildings, and a lot of the ex-servicemen just sort of turned them into barracks; they sort of bunked there. Garages that were to be torn down that were vacant—they took over these garages, had no respect for private property, didn't even ask permission of the owners—they didn't know who the hell the owners were. They would march; they would hold midnight vigils around the White House . . . they would march around the White House practically in shifts. They were ordered out of Washington four or five times, and they refused. The one that they did get to shove these bedraggled ex-servicemen out of Washington was none other than the great Douglas MacArthur. But when these ex-soldiers wouldn't move, they poked them with their bayonets, or hit them on the head with the butt of the rifle. As night fell, they were given orders to get out, and they refused, and they crossed there, and the soldiers set those shanties that these people were living in on fire. So the bonus marchers straggled back to the various places they came from without their bonus.

KITTY MCCULLOCH: There were many beggars and people that would come to your back door, and they'd say they were hungry. Well, I wouldn't give them money because I didn't have it. But I did take them in and put 'em in my kitchen and give them something to eat. Well, this one man came; it was right before Christmas. And my husband had had a suit tailored . . . and it was a very nice suit, so he put it to one side; he didn't wear it for ordinary. And I thought he didn't like the suit, because it had hung there, you know. So this man . . . I said, "Well, your clothes are all ragged. I think I have a nice suit for you." So I gave him this suit, and the following Sunday, my husband wanted to go to a wake . . . And it was a black suit with a little fine, white stripe in it, and he said, "Where's my good suit?" And I said, "Well, Daddy, you never wore it so I . . . I . . . Well, it's gone." He says, "Where is it gone?" And I said, "Well, I gave it to a man that had such shabby clothes, and he didn't have any. Anyway you've got three other suits, and I think that he didn't have any, so I gave it to him." He said, "You're the limit, Mother." He said, "I . . . I . . . I just can't understand you."

EMMA TILLER: The whites in the South is like they is I guess most other places. They will not give and help. Especially the ones who has turned out to be tramps and hobos. They come to their door for food, they will drive them away. White tramps, they will drive them away. But, if a Negro come, they will feed him. They always go and get something or other and give him something to eat . . . and they'll even give them a little money. They'll ask 'em and say, you know, "Do you smoke, or do you dip snuff, or do you use anything like that?" "Yes, ma'am. Yes, ma'am." Well they would give 'em a quarter or fifty cents, you know, and give him a little sack of food and a bar of soap or somethin' like that. Well, but they own color, they wouldn't do that for 'em. And then the Negro woman would say, you know, "Well, we got some cold food in there we can give 'em." She'd say, "Oh, no, don't give 'em nothin'; he'll be back tomorrow," you know. So they won't bestow—

Oh, you mean the Negro woman who works for the white mistress, the wife?

EMMA TILLER: Yes, yes, yes. She would take food and put it in a bag and sometimes wrap it in newspaper, and would hurry out, and sometimes would have to run down the alley because he'd be gone down the alley, and holler at him, "Hey, mister!" And he would stop, you know, and said, "Come here." And he'd come back, and said, "Look, you come back by after a while, and I'll put some food out there in a bag and I'll set it downside the can so that you don't see it." If we could see soap, we'd swipe a bar of soap and a face rag or somethin' or other, you know, and stick it in there for 'im. Negroes *always* was feeding these tramps. Even sometimes we would see them on the railroad tracks picking up stuff, and we would tell 'em, you know, to come to our house, and give them the address, and tell them to come by; that we would give them an old shirt or a pair of pants or some old shoes . . . and some food. We always would give them food.

Many times I have gone in my house and taken my husband's old shoes and his coat, and some of them, he needed them himself, but I didn't feel he needed them as bad as that man needed them, because that man, to me, was in a worse shape than he was in. Regardless of whether it was Negro or white, I would give 'em to him.

[strains of "Hard Travelin' " playing]

SIDNEY WEINBERG: October twenty-ninth, nineteen hundred and twenty-nine [the day of the crash]. I was down all night long, and I think I stayed in the office a week without going home. The tape was running, I've forgotten how long at night. I think the New York Stock Exchange ticker tape—it was ten or eleven o'clock at night before we got the final reports of what was done.

Remember what the men were talking about, the people, their feelings?

SIDNEY WEINBERG: Well, by that time they were so stunned they were thinking anything. They didn't know what it was all about. 'Cause it came out like a thunderclap out of the air.

You had general confusion all throughout the street, because they didn't understand it any more than anybody else. They thought something would be announced. It got so serious that very prominent people were making statements. Like Mr. John D. Rockefeller Jr., who was making a statement on the steps, I think it was, of J. P. Morgan & Co., that he and his sons were buying common stocks, which . . . immediately the market went down again.

A lot of people were hurt. Why, people were literally jumping out the window. Franklin D. Roosevelt showed real leadership and courage. And we were on the verge of having the change of our whole system if he hadn't done what he did.

FDR saved the system, in my opinion. You'd have had . . . The Depression would have been much deeper and it . . . it's trite to say that the system would go out the window. Certainly a lot of the institutions of the system were changed anyway in the normal course of it. But it could be much worse. You could have had rebellion.

CLIFFORD BURKE: Listen, truthfully, the average Negro don't know such a thing as Depression. Because from the day he was born, he was born in depression . . . so naturally, he don't know no more than the word "depression." As far as a job was concerned, the best he could get would be a job, like I say, driving team, or working in a coal yard, working in some factory. If he was in a factory, he was the janitor or the porter, which didn't pay much. So you can understand very clearly why no such thing as the Depression really meant too much to him.

Then another thing, if you figure it up this way, the advantage that we had as Negroes was this: our wives and our mothers, they could go to the store and get a bag of beans, and maybe a bag of potatoes, and a big sack of flour, and a big piece of fat meat. And they could cook this up and we could eat it. You take the other fella—I'm referring now to the white fella. He couldn't afford . . . he couldn't do this . . . for the simple reason was this here: He'd always been in a position where he could get something good to eat. His wife would tell him, "Look if you can't do better than this here, I'm gonna leave you." I mean, this is real; I seen it happen, see. You take a fella had a job, say, paying him sixty dollars a week, and here I'm making twenty. Now, if I go home and take some beans or anything home to my wife, she'll fix that, we'll sit down, and we'll eat it. It isn't exactly what we want, but we'll eat it. But this white fella that's been making this big money, and he go bring this home, and his wife isn't going to accept this. [Chuckles]

Why did these fellas—all these big wheels—why did they kill themselves? They weren't able to really live up to the standards that they'd been living up to before. The American white man has been superior so long, until it's just something that he can't figure out why he should come back and come down . . . He can't understand this. He couldn't stand the idea of being defeated, see. And when I say defeated, he couldn't stand the idea of having to go on relief like the Negro had to go. He couldn't stand to think that he had to work for a small salary, and as I said before, bring home the beans instead of bringing home a steak.

I can remember very distinctly a friend of mine who just before the Depression was pretty well set. And by them not knowing that he was a Negro, he got tied up downtown in stocks . . . and he came back home and drank poison and it killed him. I think he had about twenty thousand dollars that he blew in the stock market. It was a rarity, though, to hear tell of a Negro killing himself over a financial situation. Well, I can understand very clearly why he didn't do it, because there were so few that had anything that had to do it, see. [Laughs]

JOE MORRISON: We was used to rough times . . . always. I went to Detroit and worked a little while. I got fired for . . . over a grievance in 'thirty-four. Well, I got a couple of jobs, but they had me blacklisted, and I didn't get anything . . . [Small laugh] I never got a job again until I went to work in the steel mill in 'thirty-six. And these people here that are getting pretty fair wages wouldn't be . . . again, and if somebody hadn't put up a fight for it a long time ago. That's the thing about it that's forgotten. The difference I see is that there's fewer of them educated on . . . on labor.

For as far back as I can remember, up until since the end of World War II, you always found a bunch of young workers, up and coming, that read a lot and kept up with the times. And they could . . . they liked to discuss history and things like that. The people has forgotten a lot. They just . . . the young generation has just simply forgotten, and the history of these periods back of us is just being covered up.

EVELYN FINN: I find a human being forgets very easy. They flare up very easy, and they forget very easy. If they get a little prosperity, they don't know—they don't know nothing about what's in the past. Even I think with wars and everything . . . they forget. They even forget when they lose somebody in the war. I don't think it affects them too much.

I went and worked in New Orleans a year . . . it was in 'thirty-three, the summer of 'thirty-three. And there had been a union there, but it didn't mean nothing. You know how unions get there. . . . They didn't do anything, either. So we went to work, and there was a couple more girls, and so we went up to the council, the union council, to try to get help to organize the women workers in these shops making men's clothing. And I even got up to the councilmen one day, and they kept hee-hawing and you know, trying to . . . Thought we were women that didn't know what we were doing. And so I got up one night, one day, and I said, "Well, listen, I want to see one man in here that's got a union label in his clothes." And that made 'em mad. We got fired. [Chuckles] And the wages they were working for . . . Well, that's where I got the experience of my life. But in Saint Louis, before there was a union, I took out shops! Oh, yes, I'd take 'em out.

When you took out shops, how do you mean?

EVELYN FINN: They got a union.

How would you do that?

EVELYN FINN: Well, you just organize your workers. You first have to get 'em on your side, you know. And then you challenge the boss! The girls used to come in, in the morning, and they'd be tired. I said, "Well, I come in to fight today. Don't make no difference to me whether I work or not." [Laughs]

[Strains of "Roll the Union On" playing, followed by strains of "The Farmer Is the Man"]

OSCAR HELINE: After he'd lived all his life on a given farm, he lost it. It was taken away from him . . . just one after the other. And it got so that the farmers couldn't stand it anymore. They had seen their neighbors sold out.

Now, during this period of time, we'd had lots of trouble on the highway. Some people were so determined that they could correct this by withholding produce from the market, particularly in northwest Iowa. We had farmers who would organize themselves, and they would man the highways. And those who would want to sell produce would be stopped, and the produce dumped on the highway. Cream cans were emptied in the ditches, and eggs were dumped on the highways. Normally they would never react like this except in desperation. And those of us who had been brought up as conservatives, which most of us were, didn't find it easy to go out and do these things.

Right at that time was being burned—it was cheaper than coal—corn was being burned. We burned a little here. We didn't like to, but it was cheaper than coal. You couldn't haul it to town and trade it for coal. In other words, we burned it, and you might as well let it lay because it wouldn't pay any bills. You couldn't hardly buy groceries with a ten-cent corn. It would hardly pay for the transportation, you see. We had situations out in South Dakota where the price listed in the country elevator was minus three cents. If you wanted to sell them a bushel of corn, you also had to bring in three cents a bushel in cash . . . or they couldn't afford to take it. They couldn't pay the transportation and handling.

So you see how desperate this thing is. And then when the federal government came out with these funds . . . That was the hope; that was the new hope; that was the *real* hope.

The real boost came when we got into the Second World War. And the beginnings of it, of course, created hope. I had a neighbor over here during this period when we were just getting out of the Depression and prices weren't very good. And we had a boy that was ready to go to service . . . and one day he told me that what we needed in this country was a damn good war. And I said yes, but I hate to pay with the price of my son. Which we did . . . [A long pause; he chokes up]

[*Softly*] *Oh, God.*

OSCAR HELINE: It's too much to pay . . . and I think we're too smart a people to let that happen again. I don't think we have to go to war to have prosperity . . .

EMIL LORIKS: Five hundred farmers came marching up Capitol Hill one day. It just thrilled me. I didn't know that farmers were intelligent enough to organize to come to our state capital here in Marston . . . Capitol Hill. Well, it signified a lot of strength that I didn't realize we had. The potential there for action. And so this kept going and I just . . . And the day after the farmers left, a senator from Lake County, the adjoining county, got up and attacked 'em. He said they were a radical bunch of—he called them anarchists and Bolsheviks and so on, he said. [Laughs] And there was a banner, he said, that was redder than anything in Moscow, Russia. And I thought, what was that banner? It was a piece of muslin hung up in the auditorium that says: "We Buy Together, We Sell Together, We Hold Together."

The Holiday Association was organized as an emergency organization in thirty-one. Its purpose was to withhold farm products from the market for cost of production. We were hoping to get legislation that would ensure cost of production. And this took hold . . . It spread like a prairie fire. It crossed the border into South Dakota. There was a spirit of militancy. The slogan was—this was the slogan I heard: "Neither Buy nor Sell, and Let the Taxes Go to Hell." [Chuckles]

First sale, or real dramatic one, was at Millbank, South Dakota. They moved in to sell a farmer out, and the Holiday boys moved in, in force . . . and they bid the stuff in for a nickel or a dime. If somebody really started to bid that wanted to buy something, they'd just elbow 'em out, says, "You don't know . . . You get out; you move out of here. Move aside." And at Millbank they had the sheriff and about sixteen deputies there. And one of them got a little trigger happy, which was a mistake, and the boys disarmed him so fast, they didn't know what happened. They just yanked their belt; they didn't even unbuckle them. They took their guns away from them. And a leader up there by the name of Oscar Brekke got up and made quite a speech. We called him the Patrick Henry of the movement. And he made a speech deploring violence. And he deplored the fact that the sheriff and his deputies came in there to a peaceful assembly and started this ruckus. He got up on a manure spreader and made this speech. [Chuckles] That dramatized this thing all over.

After that sale we didn't have much trouble stopping sales. Farmers would crowd into the courthouse, probably five, six hundred . . . and it made it impossible for the officers to carry out the sales. [Chuckles] They tell me of an incident on [Highway] 75, they were coming in there, and one lone farmer come out of the woods, and he had big planks across the road . . . and they ordered him to move those planks, you know. He said, "I'm not. . . . You're not going through." Well, they came out there with their guns and pointed at him, and he said, "Go ahead and shoot, but there isn't going to be a one of you SOBs get out of here alive." [Chuckles] There was probably fifteen hundred farmers there in, around in the woods. So they didn't get through.

It's almost like the American Revolution in a way, isn't it?

EMIL LORIKS: Yeah. It was so close to it . . . it was so close to it.

BUDDY BLANKENSHIP: I went to work in the mines. I was about fifteen or sixteen years old, and I had about fourteen miles to go to school. . . . I had to walk it. . . . And I told my dad, "I ain't goin' to school no more." Well, he said, "If you don't want to go to school, why, you just come on and go to work with me." I went in the mines and went to work. We was on horseback all the way there. Many times, why, I'd be sitting behind my dad and get off and hammer his feet out of the stirrups . . . they'd be froze so tight in the stirrups. Well, we got up at five o'clock every morning. . . . We started work at five o'clock every morning. Had to be at the mines at six . . . and we got out at ten at night. That's sixteen, seventeen hours. The boss said we had to clean it up. If we didn't clean it up, there'd be another man in the place the next morning to clean it up. Just stay there till we did clean up.

BUDDY BLANKENSHIP: You had to get on your knees. Coal was slow. And I've traveled hard seven miles for the man, traveled back and forth, seven miles . . . on my knees. Well, I've had my knees to be swelled up to be . . . with big knots on 'em, big as double fists.

I liked the mines; I liked the mines, until I got so I couldn't work in 'em. And I can't get in 'em now, you see. Last I got in 'em, when I worked in 'em, why they was . . . my wind was too short and there's too much dead air . . . and I just choked up. I couldn't do no good in 'em. I couldn't work too long in 'em no more.

MARY OWSLEY: When he went to work in the coal mines, he worked for the Norton Coal Company at Nortonville, Kentucky. And he fired the boilers . . . and then he was a very good dynamite man. And then when the shift come out, he'd go down and chute down the coal. And he went to work one day and he noticed on the side of the boiler a place about as big as a saucer, where it was . . . they call it a breather. It's a weak place on the boiler. And he come in that night and he says, "Well, I'll go back to work Monday, but I may not stay; I may come back home." Because he had told Mr. Ball that that had to be fixed . . . because he didn't want to get killed. He had his family . . . he didn't want to get killed.

So he went back to work then, Monday . . . went along. Then I saw him coming back home. They hadn't fixed it. . . . They hadn't done a *thing* about it. And he told 'em, he said, "In less than three weeks there'll be an explosion." And sure enough there was. Killed three men and two mine mules . . . from that very thing. But he left. But we had bought our furniture from the company store. We lived in a company house. . . . I had to buy every gallon of water I used. They undermined their employees so bad . . . they ruined all the water wells. And we didn't live extravagant, either; believe me, we didn't. But I've seen him have to borry from his next paycheck . . . what they call scrip . . . to buy just medicine and things like that . . . till the next payday. And we bought—we paid two hundred and . . . over two hundred dollars, two hundred and sixty-some-odd dollars for furniture from the coal mine company, and we paid it all back but twenty dollars. And when he went up and got a job around Greenville, Kentucky, near Central City, he brought a truck back down there to get the furniture, and they took the whole thing away from us. They wouldn't let us have it and let him pay the twenty dollars. They took the furniture.

Because he was a troublemaker?

MARY OWSLEY: *No*, not because he was a troublemaker . . . because he quit his job there where that breather was on that boiler. That's the kind of troublemaker he was, you're mighty right he was. . . . He wanted to live!

[Strains of "Sixteen Tons" play]

JANE YODER: I don't know. . . . I guess you just struggle. I guess you just struggle for survival . . . survival just to be warm. You can have bread . . . and that Karo syrup was a treat.

I remember this incident of that Indian blanket coat . . . Oh! Because Katie came home with it, and had it in her clothes closet for quite a while . . . and I didn't have a coat. And I can remember putting on that coat, and it was so warm, and how I thought, Oh, this is marvelous, gee. And I waited till Sunday and I wore it to church, and then everybody laughed. I looked *horrid.* Here was this black-haired kid with a tendency to be overweight. . . . My God, when I think of that coat. But I wore that coat, laugh or not; I was warm. And I can remember thinking, To hell with it! I don't care what . . . Doesn't mean a thing, finally. You've laughed, laugh hard . . . you'll get it out of your system. It's a brand-new coat and it's *warm.* I'm warm!

Yes, I remember going without food. I can think of . . . We'd have bread . . . and no money anywhere. No money anywhere. And, oh, when I . . . It just overwhelms me sometimes when I think of those two younger brothers who would work to get some food and maybe go to the store. But they would see this nine-hundred-dollar grocery bill, you know [Chuckles] . . . and just couldn't do it . . . until that youngest brother . . . We all laugh now because we all say, "Remember Frankie?" Frankie's "*Tu costa puno.*" Anything you brought in the house that was food, *tu costa puno. Tu costa puno* is "Did it cost a lot?" [A Croation phrase] No matter what you brought in, you know . . . if you brought bread and eggs and Karo syrup. I don't remember so much my going to the store and buying food. I must have been terribly proud and, and felt . . . I can't do it. But how early we all stayed away from going to the store. Because we sensed that my father didn't have the money and so we stayed hungry.

And then I can think of when the WPA—Works Progress Administration—came in. And my father immediately got employed on the WPA. And I remember how stark it was for me to come into training and have girls, one of them who lived across the hall from me at Patton Memorial, whose father was a doctor in Michigan . . . I can think of the people and how it struck me of their . . . *their* impression of the WPA. Because without, before I could ever say my father was employed on the WPA, discussions and bull sessions in our rooms, immediately it was, "These lazy people that don't do a thing, the shovel leaners," and . . . and, and I'd just sit there and listen to them. And then I'd look around, and I realized, sure, her father's a doctor in Saint Joe, Michigan. Well, how nice. In my family there was no respectable employment, there was no . . . until I thought: You don't know what it's *like*.

My father survived the Depression. The war came along and he went to work in a defense plant in Seneca, Illinois. And my father was always *happy* to have a job and start making money. Oh, I don't think of anything that stood out for my father like, you know, "Yemen dillo" . . . I have work. This man was really happy to be working.

ROBIN LANGSTON: My father had a restaurant. This was in Arkansas. And when I knew the Depression had really hit with full impact . . . the electric lights went off. My parents could no longer pay the one-dollar electric bill, which it amounted to maybe for a month or two months. A dollar-eighty at the most. And kerosene lamps went up in the home and in the business. Over each individual table in the restaurant there was a kerosene lamp. This did something to me. Because it let me know that my father wasn't the greatest cat in the world, and I had always thought he was, you know. But it also let me know that he could adjust to any situation, and he taught us how to adjust to situations.

Now, we were fortunate compared to the situations of other people. We always had food. There was never any money, but who needed money then? The restaurant went right through the Depression; we were selling hamburgers for a nickel. My father would sell a meal ticket. You could get a full-course meal—that is meat and three vegetables—for twenty-five cents. I remember distinctly feeding little snotty-nosed white kids. My father and mother just did this out of the goodness of their hearts. There were . . . I guess there must have been ten white families within fifty feet of us. I remember feeding them. I remember my parents feeding little black kids. I remember when the times got so hard the sheriff pawned a radio to my father for ten dollars. This was a white sheriff, a white official, who had to come to a black man to get ten dollars. The reason he needed the ten dollars, he had some people out of town, he wanted to bring them there to eat some chicken. And this was during the time when a lot of the black young people wanted to venture out and go places, and they were afraid to hobo then, because they didn't want to be caught up in a Scottsboro thing. They knew about the Scottsboro case and about the lynching. They knew they had a lynching in Mississippi and the lynchings in Alabama. We also knew in school that Tuskegee Institute or Fisk Library—one used to keep a report on all lynchings. One year there were about two thousand lynchings, and they documented each lynching. Yeah, we knew all about that.

I think a Depression could come again, but I think it would behoove the federal government not to let it come, because you're dealing with a different breed of cattle now. See, now, if they really want anarchy, let a Depression come now. My sixteen-year-old son is not the person I was when I was six-teen. He's an adult at sixteen. He's working in a department store and going to school, too. And he has manly responsibilities and he doesn't want any shit. These kids now do not want it. When I was sixteen, I wasn't afraid to die, but the kid sixteen now is not afraid to kill.

[Strains of "God Bless the Child" playing]

JEROME ZERBE: From 1935 to 1939, I worked at El Morocco, and I invented a thing which has become a pain in the neck to most people. I took photographs of the fashionable people and sent them to the papers. They were really the top, top social. And what do you mean by society? That's difficult to define. These were the people whose houses one knew were filled with treasures. These were the women who dressed the best. These were the women who had the most beautiful of all jewels. These were the dream people that we all looked up to and hoped that we, or our friends, could sometimes know and be like.

Did you ever talk about what happened outside? There were breadlines. There were various other things occurring. Not too nice, you know.

JEROME ZERBE: As I remember, I don't think they ever mentioned them . . . never socially. Because I've always had a theory: When you're out with friends, out socially, everything must be charming . . . and you don't allow the ugly. We don't even discuss the Negro question.

What was happening around the city? Do you remember the . . . people talking of breadlines, or Hoovervilles, or apple sellers?

JEROME ZERBE: No, there were none of those. Not in New York. Never. Never. There were a few beggars.

New Deal?

JEROME ZERBE: New Deal. Well that was an invention of Franklin Roosevelt's. And it meant absolutely nothing except higher taxation . . . and that he did.

The thirties . . . society . . . our last images . . .

JEROME ZERBE: It was a glamorous, glittering moment.

WARD JAMES: I, well, I lived off friends. I had one very good friend who cashed in all his bonus bonds to pay his rent, and he had an extra bed, so he let me sleep there. I finally went on relief, which was an experience I wouldn't want anybody else ever to go through in New York City. A single man going on relief at that particular time was just . . . Well, it comes as close to crucifixion as you can do it without actual mechanical details. Well, it was 'thirty-five or 'thirty-six, in that area. It was after I lost my job with the publishing house, and I needed whatever money I could get anywhere. The interview was to me utterly ridiculous and mortifying. Well, in the middle of it, a more dramatic guy than I was plunged down the stairways— 'cause we were on the second floor—head first, to demonstrate that he was going to get on relief if he had to go to a hospital to do it. [Chuckles]

It was questions like: "Well, what have you been living on?"
"Well, I borrowed some money."
"Who'd you borrow it from?"
"Friends."

"Who are your friends? Where have you been living?"

"I've been living with friends."

"Well . . ."

I wish I could recall the whole thing. This went on for a half an hour or something. I finally turned to the young man who was interviewing me and said, "I've been talking about friends. Do you happen to know what a friend is?" And a little after that I got my . . . at least the interview was over. I did get certified sometime later. I've been trying to remember how much they paid. It seems to me it was nine dollars a month. I suppose there's some reason back of it. I'm a single man. . . . Why, why didn't I have a family? I took my family west to Ohio, where they could live simply.

I came away feeling like I hadn't any business even living any longer. I was imposing on somebody's great society, or something like that. [Chuckles]

EILEEN BARTH: I remember one of the first families I visited. This was a family from somewhere in Illinois, who had come to Chicago because I think this man was a railroad man. He was a Scotsman. I'm not sure I remember all the details, but I do have a picture of this man because of something that happened.

I was told by my supervisor that when I went out to the home to investigate that I really had to see the poverty, that I had to know exactly what this family needed, and what they lacked. So I was told that I should investigate to see how much clothing they had on hand if they asked for clothing. Well, I looked in this man's closet because I . . . this was what I was told to do, that I should look in the closets. And this man was tall, well built. . . . I don't know why I think he had gray hair because he wasn't terribly old. But this is what I remember about him. And I think he'd been a railroad man and had always worked. Lost his job on the railroad, came to Chicago with his family to get work. I don't think he found work . . . so they were stranded here.

They lived in another county so they didn't qualify for permanent relief here, but only for temporary assistance until we could verify their residence . . . somewhere in central Illinois, I believe. And, ah [Sighs] . . . he let me look in the closet . . . [Holding back sobs] . . . and . . . I'm just crying to think about it. But he was so insulted . . . he was so insulted to think that I would do this. . . . I'm trying to remember. I remember this feeling of . . . of . . . of humiliation. I sensed this terrible humiliation. I think he said, "Well, do you really have to look in the closet? I really haven't anything to hide." I think that's what he said. But I could see that he was very proud. He was deeply humiliated . . . and I was, too.

VIRGINIA DURR: In Jefferson County about four-fifths of the people were on relief. And there was no government relief. So this meant that they had this—just this two dollars and a half a week that the Red Cross provided them, and that they could beg, borrow, or steal.

But the thing that also struck me as being so terrible was that, just the way my mother and father had this terrible feeling of shame and guilt, and it was their failure they'd lost all their property, these people had the same feeling of shame and guilt who had lost their jobs. They didn't blame the United States still; they'd didn't blame the capitalist system; they just blamed themselves. And they thought . . . Well, you know, they would say in the most apologetic way, "Well, you know, if we hadn't bought that radio . . . or if we hadn't bought that old second-hand car . . . or if we'd saved our money and . . ." You know, they really blamed themselves. And it was just this terrible feeling they had of shame because they were on relief.

PEGGY TERRY: When we'd come home from school in the evening, my mother would send us to the soup line . . . and we were never allowed to cut. But after we'd been going to the soup line for about a month, we'd go down there, and if you happened to be one of the first ones in line, you didn't get anything but the water that was on top. So we'd ask the guy that was ladling out the soup into the bucket . . . everybody had to bring their own bucket to get the soup . . . and he'd dip the greasy watery stuff off the top, and so we'd ask him to please dip down so we could get some meat and potatoes from the bottom of the kettle. And he wouldn't do it. So then we learned to cuss and we'd say, "Dip down, God damn it!" And then we'd go across the street, and one place had bread, large loaves of bread, and then down the road just a little piece was a big shed, and they gave milk. And my sister and me would take two buckets each, and we'd bring one back full of soup and one back full of milk and two loaves of bread each . . . and that's what we lived on for the longest time.

I remember it was fun. It was fun going to the soup line because we all went down the road and we laughed and we played. And the only thing that we felt was we were hungry and we were going to get food. And nobody made us feel ashamed . . . there just wasn't any of that back then. I'm not sure how the rich felt. I think the rich were as contemptuous of the poor then as they are now. But at least among the people that I knew and came in contact with, we all had a sense of understanding that it wasn't our fault . . . that it was something that had happened to the machinery. And in fact most people blamed Hoover. I mean they cussed him up one side and down the other. It was all his fault. I'm not saying he's blameless, but I'm not saying either that it was all his fault, because our system doesn't run just by one man, and it doesn't fall just by one man, either.

How much schooling do you have?

PEGGY TERRY: Sixth grade.

And what'd you do after sixth grade? You got married at fifteen.

PEGGY TERRY: Yes. Well, my husband and me started traveling around. That was just kind of our background, and we just kind of continued it. We went down in the valley of Texas, where it's very beautiful. . . . We were migrant workers down there. We picked oranges and grapefruits and lemons and limes in the Rio Grande Valley.

I was pregnant when we first started hitchhiking, and people were really very nice to us. Sometimes they would feed us, and then sometimes we would . . . I remember the one time we slept in a haystack and the lady of the house came out and found us, and she says, "Well, this is really very bad for you because you're going to have a baby." And she says, "You need a lot of milk." So she took us up to the house and she had a lot of rugs hanging on the clothesline because she was doing her housecleaning. And we told her we'd beat the rugs, you know, for her giving us the food. And she said no, she didn't expect that; that she just wanted to feed us. And we said no, that we couldn't take it unless we worked for it. So she let us beat her rugs, and I think that she had a million rugs, and we cleaned them. And then we went in and she had a beautiful table just all full of all kind of food and milk. And then when we left, she filled a gallon bucket full of milk and we took it with us. And you don't find that now. I think maybe if you did that now you'd get arrested. I think somebody'd call the police.

I think maybe the atmosphere since the end of the second war . . . Because all kind of propaganda has been going on . . . It just seems like the minute the war ended the propaganda started, and making people hate each other . . . not just hate Russians and Chinese and Germans, it was to make us hate each other, I think.

I think during the Depression, if the government had tried to do to a country what we're doing now to Vietnam, I think the people would have marched right up there and snatched Roosevelt out by the hair of his head, and shook him around. And I think maybe the whole atmosphere was created to separate people and make them suspicious of each other, and just stir a hatred of one human for another.

This may sound impossible, but do you know, if there's one thing that started me thinking, it was President Roosevelt's cuff links. I read in the paper about how many pairs of cuff links he had, and it told that some of them were rubies and all precious stones . . . these were his cuff links. And I just wondered . . . I'll never forget, I was sitting on an old tire out in the front yard, and we were hungry and *so* poor. And I was sitting out there in the hot sun—there weren't any trees—and I was wondering why it was that one man could have all those cuff links when we couldn't even have enough to eat. When we lived on gravy and biscuits. And I think maybe that was my first thought of wondering why . . . That's the first thing I remember ever wondering why.

But one thing I did want to say about when my father finally got his bonus, he bought a secondhand car for us to come back to Kentucky in. And my dad said to us kids, "All of you

get in the car. I want to take you and show you something."
And on the way over there, he talked about how rough life had
been for us. And he said, "If you think it's been rough for us,"
he said, "I want you to see people that really had it rough."
This was in Oklahoma City. And he took us to one of the
Hoovervilles . . . and that was the most incredible thing. Here
were all these people living in old rusted-out car bodies. I
mean, that was their home. There were people living in shacks
made out of orange crates. One family, with a whole lot of
kids, were living in a piano box. And here this—this wasn't
just a little section; this was an area maybe ten miles wide and
ten miles long. People living in whatever they could, jammed
together.

And when I read *Grapes of Wrath*, that was like reliving my
life. And particularly the part in there about where they lived in
this government camp. Because when we were picking fruit in
Texas, we lived in a government place like that, a government-
owned place, in Robstown, Texas. And they came around and
they helped the women make mattresses. See, we didn't have
anything. And they showed us how to sew and make dresses.
And every Saturday night we'd have a dance. And when I was
reading *Grapes of Wrath*, this was just like my life. And . . . and
I never was so proud of poor people before as I was after I
read that book.

VIRGINIA DURR: The Depression affected people in two different ways. One was—and I think this is the overwhelming
majority—and that was that having faced the terror of the lack
of a job, and the shame of having lived on relief, and the panic
of not knowing whether you were going to be able to get work
or not. . . . I think the great majority of the people reacted by,
you know, thinking that money was the most important thing

in the world. And that the most important thing to do was to get—get yours . . . and get it for your children . . . and be sure that you had it and your children had it. And nothing else mattered but getting you some money and some property, and not having this terror ever come on you again of not being able to feed your family.

On the other hand, I think there were a small number of people who felt like the whole system was lousy, and that you had to change the system. Well, now, I'm not so sure that I know what kind of a system to put in its place. I do think you've got to have a system of government that's responsive to the needs of the people.

PEGGY TERRY: I don't think people were put on earth to suffer. I think that's a lot of nonsense. I think we are the highest development on the earth, and I think we were put here to live and be happy and enjoy everything that's here. I don't think it's right for a handful of people to get ahold of all the things that make living a joy instead of a sorrow. When you wake up in the morning and the minute consciousness hits you, it's just like a big hand takes ahold of your heart and squeezes it, because you don't know what that day's gonna bring. A hunger, or . . . you just don't know. It's really—it's really hard to . . . to talk about the Depression because what can you say except you were hungry.

[More strains of "God Bless the Child" playing]

BORN TO LIVE, 1961

One of my guests, the day of my interview with Myoka Harubasa, was the skipper of The Golden Rule, *a ship sponsored by the American Friends Service Committee, the Quakers.* The Golden Rule *had been skirting the waters of the world, defying all barriers, calling out for an end to bombings such as Hiroshima and Nagasaki. My interview guest, Myoka Harubasa, was a hibakusha. Hibakusha means a survivor of Hiroshima and Nagasaki, whose life to many is worse than any death could be. There was also an interpreter from Chicago, Joan Takada, who translated for the hibakusha. Two other guests were casual visitors, seated in the studio: a Danish former staff member, Vreni Naess, who was visiting with her two-year old baby, Eric. And that was it. The hibakusha is describing a sunny morning in August 1945, and toward the end the interpreter says "I can't go on."*

[WE HEAR Myoka Harubasa speaking, followed by Joan Takada translating her words.]

MYOKA HARUBASA OF HIROSHIMA: They were looking up in the sky, trying to spot the airplane. And then she thought that there was a very big flash in the sky, so she hid her face on the ground. Then she remembers that she must have been blown away by the impact . . . and when she regained consciousness she couldn't find most of her friends. They were either blown to bits, or burned, or . . . She says that all her clothes were torn away except the very undergarment. And her skin where she has all her burns—the skin was just peeled off and hanging from her body. And she has that on her arms and legs and on her face . . . [Long pause] And she said it was such an intense heat that she jumped into the nearby river. . . . the small river that was running through the city. . . . She says that her friends who were in the river . . . [Pause; slight sob from the interpreter.] I don't think I can say it.

[Japanese children singing a Japanese children's song segues into American children singing an American children's song]

MAN AT DINNER TABLE: The fact that you find a nine- or ten-year-old child being gravely concerned about the fact that he's not going to be living in ten or fifteen years because of this atomic war that's coming up is . . . is . . . this is the frightening part to me. Heck, when I was nine or ten years old, I was wondering if . . .

WOMAN AT DINNER TABLE: You were greedy!

MAN: Jesus! Is the pond going to have polliwogs in it this year or not, you know, something like this. But here these kids are wondering: Am I going to be alive?

WOMAN: It bothers them. It really does. And to have these remarks come out at home out of a clear blue sky: "I wish I'd never been born." Oh! It's frightening. No, she just said, "Well, if the bomb is going to hit, I'm going to enjoy life while I can. I'll do what I please." Oh, what an answer! And what do you say?

SECOND MAN AT DINNER TABLE: And how old is she, ten?

WOMAN: Nine.

MAN: Nine.

[American children singing]

> God said to Noah, There's gonna be a floody, floody
> God said to Noah, There's gonna be a floody, floody
> Get those children out of the muddy, muddy
> Children of the Lord

PERRY MIRANDA: Well, remember, we talked a little about the guys thinking over different things. Y'know, putting down their head sometimes, and going back, say, thinking over some memories. Well, what do you think? What are some of the things they think about, or what are some of the things they worry about? [Pause] What are some of the things that the guys worry about?

YOUTH: I don't know, man.

MIRANDA: Do you ever worry about what's gonna happen to you when you grow older?

YOUTH: We was born to die; that's all.

MIRANDA: You were born to die?

YOUTH: Yeah.

MIRANDA: What about in between the time you're born and the time you die?

[Pete Seeger strumming Beethoven's Ninth on his banjo]

Born to die? What about in between the time you're born and the time you die? [Strumming continues under Terkel's voice.] Man is a long time coming. To paraphrase the old Chicago poet:

Man may yet win.
Brother may yet line up with brother.
Who can live without hope?
In the darkness with a great bundle of grief, the people
   march.
In the night, and overhead a shovel of stars for keeps,
   the people march.
Where to. What next?"

[Sound of drums and bells]

Two drummers, on the island of Ceylon, engaged in percussive battle.

T. P. AMERASINGHE: That's a favorite pastime of the people on a Sunday afternoon—after work, for example. You will find drums playing, drummers trying to outdo one another.

How does the audience decide who wins—by the applause?

AMERASINGHE: No, they themselves come together. That's the beauty of it. The two drummers, finding that they cannot be . . . one cannot outdo the other, play a final duet together.

Oh, that's marvelous! It isn't a question of one beating another.

AMERASINGHE: No, no, no.

They finally meet and they merge their strengths, fuse their strengths, or their arts.

AMERASINGHE: I think that's also an old tradition of a comradely feeling, you see. You have the competition, but at the end both meet on equal terms.

[Drummers drumming]

An American art critic, observing a Goya hanging in the Prado.

ALEXANDER ELIOT: This picture of the two men clobbering each other in the quicksand in the valley, at the Prado, is first of all a horrible picture; a shocking picture. After that you begin to see it within the context of this magnificent landscape: all a silver, somber, magnificently harmonious thing . . . [A cello plays under his words.] and in the midst of it are these two bloody idiots. And you see that if you could only get through to them somehow, and tell them what they're doing, and how they are denying by their very action the beauty and the harmony and the mystery that surrounds them—they're denying the fact that they're equally brothers—somehow they would recognize what Goya so poignantly makes you realize in looking at the picture.

[Cello ends and the Weavers sing.]

> My Lord, what a morning
> My Lord, what a morning
> My Lord, what a morning
> When the stars begin to fall.

LILLIAN SMITH: My father and my mother were quite sincere in believing in human dignity, in democracy, in the Christian beliefs of brotherhood, fellowship, love, mercy, justice; that sort of thing. And yet, at the same time, they accepted what I call the ritual of segregation just as though it were something immovable. And you had to be as decent as possible, you know, within this immovable something. And so, I would go to church, and as a small child—and I was a rather critical small child—I'd hear about Christian brotherhood, and of course none of my little Negro friends were at church. And I would come home and say, "Why? Why?" And always, the questions were gently unanswered . . .

The voice of a novelist from the Deep South . . .

LILLIAN SMITH: And when I would say, "Why? Why?" and say it too much, they would say, "When you're older, you will understand." Now, that was the part where it began to really work in my mind, and I began to feel that part of my mind was segregated from another part of my mind. There was a great split there, you see. A great chasm had already entered my mind, so that I was believing something and I was not living it. And that began to disturb me very much, although in many ways, I was just a kid, just a gay, funny, and ridiculous child. But in many ways, I was asking what I always speak of as the

"Great Questions": "Who am I?" "Where am I going?"
"What is death?" "Who is God?" "Why am I here?" And
sometimes I think I worried my mother very much because I
said, "Mother, why are *you* my mother?"

Here now we all ask; children ask, and the Greeks ask, and
existential philosophers ask, and every thoughtful person:
"Who am I?"

The voice of a novelist from Paris.

SIMONE DE BEAUVOIR: When I was young, I misunderstood
the importance of the external world. I believed you can just
do what you want and think what you think by yourself. Little
by little I learned that my own ideas were the reflection of
things going around me; that my whole life was the reflection
of a lot of things going on in the world.

I was not at all a lonely person, and I did not invent and create myself. It depended mostly on circumstance. It was the war
which was a big revelation in that respect. And then, going
deeper and deeper into the experience provided by the war, I
discovered the tightness of the ties which tie me to the whole
world.

JAMES BALDWIN: The effort, it seems to me, is if you can examine and face your life, you can discover the terms in which
you are connected to other lives. And they can discover, too,
the terms in which they are connected to other people . . .

The voice of a young novelist from Harlem . . .

JAMES BALDWIN: It's happened to every one of us, I'm sure.
You know, when one has read something which you thought

only happened to you, and you discovered that it happened a hundred years ago to Dostoevsky. And this is a very great liberation for the suffering, struggling person who always thinks that he's alone.

[The Weavers sing]

> You'll weep for the rocks and the mountains
> You'll weep for the rocks and the mountains
> You'll weep for the rocks and the mountains
> When the stars begin to fall.

A singer from South Africa remembers her mother:

MIRIAM MAKEBA: Yes, she never went to school. All she did was work all her life. She started working when she was about ten years old. They used to work in—she was born in Swaziland—and to be able to live they had to work for the white man who owns the farm. They didn't get paid. They just worked for a place to live.

Yet your mother, you say, who had no schooling, no education, knew these songs?

[Makeba singing beneath her words]

MIRIAM MAKEBA: Oh, yes, she knew most of them. Some of them are not as old as she would be, but most of them are. And she . . . she used to work for these white people. She spoke very good Afrikaans, which is Dutch, and she spoke English very fluently. You would never know she never went to school.

An elderly sharecropper from Tennessee laughingly answers the question about her capacity for work:

GEORGIA TURNER: Did I cut trees? [Laughter] I wish you'd seen the trees I cut! You know, I'm gonna tell you one thing. If you think I'm not telling you truth, go in the neighborhood down there.

Now, my sister had a little boy. He named Willie Sheldon; he yet live down there on the place. And he used to haul the wood. He was about ten years old—he wasn't large enough to do much cuttin'. I'd cut, and he'd haul. And he'd give me half of the wood. I cut five loads of wood every day—five loads, and he hauled it. He hauled loads, two loads, and a half to my house and two loads and a half to his house. That's how I got my wood. I cut it! Yeah, cut big loads—couldn't hardly meet your arms around it! Wouldn't take me long. I tell you, I'm a good axman. You ought to know. You don't know what good work in me. I can yet do it! I can yet work.

And a Chicago poet quietly recalls her friend's capacity for life.

GWENDOLYN BROOKS: Vit—of course, that wasn't her name—was a friend of mine who had the irrepressibility that just seems unconfinable, even in death. And that's why I wrote:

Carried her unprotesting out of the door.
Kicked back the casket-stand. But it can't hold her,
That stuff in satin aiming to enfold her,
The lid's contrition nor the bolts before.
Oh. Oh. Too much. Too much. Even now, surmise,
She rises in the sunshine. There she goes,

Back to the bars she knew and a repose
In love-rooms and the things in people's eyes.
Too vital and too squeaking must emerge.
Even now she does the snake-hips with a hiss
Slops the bad wine across her shantung, talks
Of pregnancy, guitars and bridge work, walks
In parks or alleys, comes happily on the verge
Of happiness, haply hysterics. Is.

Oh, yeah!

[Bessie Smith singing "Gimme a Pig Foot and a Bottle of Beer"]

An operatic bosso-buffo remembers a celebrated colleague of the past, who was known for his lust for life as well as for his artistry:

SALVATORE BACCALONI: He is the most great actor—the most great personality I know in the world. When he sing the Boris, oh, yes, there are many, many Boris around. Some are good, or less good [Laughs], but Chaliapin remained the master. He go down in the street near to death. . . . I remember, he attack the *monologo* with one little breath of voice.

Chaliapin . . .

BACCALONI: [Sings] *O triste il cor* . . . He's tremble on the stage, because he is near to fall down. But many Boris today acts [Sings again, this time much louder and with less feeling] *O triste il cor* . . . What kind of sick man is this? Is no sick at all! [Big laugh]

In other words, he actually felt the role. He wasn't just a singer: he was an actor.

BACCALONI: He was no singer, he's not an actor; Chaliapin, when he play Boris, was Boris! [Laughs]

He was Boris! [Both laugh]

[The sounds of cast members of Brendan Behan's play *The Hostage*. They are discussing the author in a mood of high hilarity. Terkel points out that Behan is really saying, "There's no place on earth like the world." The cast members decide to sing this song, which Behan had written for the play.

There's no place on earth like the world
There's no place wherever you be.
There's no place on earth like the world,
That's straight up, and take it from me!

Never throw stones at your mother;
You'll be sorry for it when she's dead.
Never throw stones at your mother—
Throw bricks at your father instead!

[Pete Seeger singing "Abiyoyo"]

The voices of laughing men and laughing women. And the tellers of tales, tall and short:

PETE SEEGER: You know, once, long, long, long ago there was a little boy. And he liked to play the ukulele. Plink, plink, plink! He was always playing the ukulele all over the place. But, you know, the grown-ups say, "Get away, we're working here! Go off by yourself, you're getting in our way!"

Not only that, but the boy's father was a magician. He had a little magic wand . . . he could make things disappear . . . [Fades out]

I'm sorry to say I don't know much about telling stories. Gradually now, in my forty-one years, I've just barely learned how, just a little bit, to tell a story. But it's taken me all of this time to learn.

A child learns how to talk, and they talk all the time. A man buys an automobile and he rides and forgets how to use his legs. And the fact is, let's face it—printing was invented and a lot of people forgot how to tell stories. You don't need to tell stories to your children at night. You buy them a twenty-five-cent book at the local drugstore, or buy them a phonograph record, or switch on the radio or TV. You don't have to use your brains anymore. You don't have to make music, obviously. You don't have to be an athlete anymore. You can turn on the TV and watch the best athletes in the world use their muscles, and you sit back and grow a potbelly. You don't need to be witty anymore. You turn on the TV and watch an expert be witty. And of course the crowning shame of it all is for a man and wife to sit back and watch the expert lover pretend to make love on the little screen there.

JAMES BALDWIN: I don't ever intend to make my peace with such a world. There's something much more important than Cadillacs, Frigidaires, and IBM machines, you know. And precisely one of the things that's wrong is this notion that IBM machines and Cadillacs prove something. People are always telling me how many Negroes bought Cadillacs last year, and it terrifies me. I always wonder: Is this what you think the country is for? Do you think this is really what I came here and suffered and died for? A lousy Cadillac?

REV. WILLIAM SLOANE COFFIN JR.: Because we love the word, we pray now, oh, Father, for grace to quarrel with it, oh, thou, whose lover's quarrel with the world is the history of the world . . .

An American University chaplain offering a prayer during commencement exercises . . .

COFFIN: Grant us grace to quarrel with the worship of success and power, with the assumption that people are less important than the jobs they hold. Grant us grace to quarrel with the mass culture that tends not to satisfy, but exploit the wants of people; to quarrel with those who pledge allegiance to one race, rather than the human race. Lord, grant us grace to quarrel with all that profanes, and trivializes, and separates men.

MIRIAM MAKEBA: In South Africa if you don't have a sense of humor, it would be difficult to survive, with all that's going on there.

Every once in a while, maybe once a year, we have a big feast where we slaughter a cow, or maybe two sheep, and we cook and invite all our neighbors and the people around us to meditate to our great-grandfathers and mothers who died, and ask them to ask the Lord to help us go on living. And then the people eat and drink and they dance, and then they go back to their homes. And so . . . we sing, and we're happy . . . we try.

[Makeba singing]

WOMAN'S VOICE: After so many years, you know, in prisons, and in camp, and . . . and many years of this constant humiliation—the SS tried to convince us that there is no hope for us—we really started to believe that there was no hope for us—we really started to believe that there was no hope for us . . .

A former inmate of the Ravensbruck concentration camp . . .

WOMAN: We tried to believe that there would be a liberation someday. We tried and tried and convinced ourselves, and tried to convince the weaker ones that we were sure that the Americans or the British or the Red Army would come very soon to liberate us. But it was so long, you know. Every day for us was like a year. I think I would be right to say that we just lost hope. We tried to convince ourselves that we hoped, but we really didn't. I couldn't imagine when I could lie in a bed again—that I would have breakfast again, and lunch, and be a human being, and walk on the street and listen to music. And then, perhaps, lie in a hospital bed and die like a . . . like a normal human being.

I think they were simple people, German people, who believed that they are the *Herrenrasse*, the . . . the . . .

MAN'S VOICE: The master race.

WOMAN: The master race; they were . . . big people and we were just the . . . the

Untermenschen . . . [Fades out]

SIMONE DE BEAUVOIR: We feel we are guilty. We feel guilty because we have not the power to do what we want, or to pre-

vent ourselves from doing what we don't want, and we feel
sad because of that. And then chiefly, because we have felt the
Occupation, we have hated the Nazis when they tortured and
oppressed us, and we were in the Resistance. We don't understand: the people who have been in the Resistance now do exactly the same thing to the Algerians that the Germans did to
us. That's very difficult to understand . . . that's not under-
standable, and anyhow, we don't accept it.

[Singing "La Marseillaise"]

LILLIAN SMITH: The parts of our nature that are torn open;
the wound that must not be healed: This, in a sense, is what I
like to write about. But they would like to say, "This wound has
been healed. Therefore we don't have to even *read* anymore
about it." And this is very interesting about people, isn't it?
They want to be on the side of truth without ever facing truth.
They want to be on the side of virtue without ever knowing
what virtue is.

[The Weavers sing.]

> Oh, sinner, what will you do
> Oh, sinner, what will you do
> Oh, sinner, what will you do
> When the stars begin to fall?

[A brief recapitulation of the opening: the Japanese woman
and the translator saying, "They were looking up in the sky,
trying to spot the airplane"; the Japanese children's song; the
couple around the dinner table saying, "Heck, when I was nine
or ten years old, I was wondering if the pond would have pol-

liwogs in it this year"; once again the American children's song,
"Children of the Lord"; followed by Perry Miranda's interview with the youth, and the phrase "You were born to die,
that's all"; Beethoven's Ninth Symphony on banjo; and Terkel
repeating Miranda's question, "Born to die? What about between the time you are born and the time you die?"; and then:]

SEAN O'CASEY: That's the question, "What is life," my boy,
"What is life?" Well, I found life an enjoyable, enchanting, ac-
tive, and sometimes a terrifying experience. And I've enjoyed
it completely. A lament in one ear, maybe, but always a song in
the other. And to me, life is simply an invitation to live.

The Irish playwright who defies the calendar, and is ever young . . .

O'CASEY: You know, God, or Nature if you like, dumps a little boy at the tick of a clock, maybe, or the dawn of a day, into
life, and a tick after he dumps a little girl beside him. So the boy
and girl meet very early. And God says to the little boy; and
God says to the little girl: "Be brave. Be brave. And evermore
be brave."

SHANTA GANDHI: In one village, we had an experience
which I'll never, never forget in my life . . .

An Indian actress recalls a visit to a village during the Bengal famine.

GANDHI: It used to be our practice that after the show we
would come out and just appeal for whatever people could
give. We used to tell them, in very few words—sometimes
through song, even—extra song; we'd appeal to give whatever
they could for the people of Bengal. On one such occasion—

in a very small village it was—after the show, when we came out in the auditorium, we found there was a tremendous commotion. An old woman—she must be about fifty-five or sixty, she was bent—and she was dragging a cow right into the auditorium! I couldn't understand what was happening, and before I could recover from the surprise, she came up and said, "Take this." I had no word to say! What could I say? I said, "Well, well, well," and that's about all I could! All the speech . . . everything was gone; forgotten. It was the old woman who said, "My child, I have nothing else to give, but take this cow. It still gives milk, you know. And as you say the children are starving, without milk. Please take this. I'm an old woman; I don't need very much milk. And while I live villagers will see to it that I don't quite starve. You take this cow with you." And she insisted on giving the cow to us. What could we say? We didn't want to deprive the old woman of the cow. More than that, it would have been very difficult indeed to take the cow to Bengal. Luckily we hit on some idea, and said to her, "Grandma, please look after the cow for us 'til we are able to make some arrangement to take this cow to Bengal. It is our cow, we know, but you are *here*. And who can look after the cow better than you?" And that alone persuaded the old woman to take the cow. That was the India of that time. And we wanted to depict *that* India.

I am afraid art is very, very pale compared to real life sometimes, very pale indeed.

[Sound of sitar playing]

GEORGIA TURNER: If it takes me to lay down and get out of there and get down on my knees in that water—I had to crawl with the dogs and hogs and things—so that my children could have a better day that I had, then I don't mind doing it. And if it takes me to have to lay down and go on home to my Father, I don't mind doing that, so my children can get their freedom . . .

[Mahalia Jackson singing "Hands on the Plow"]

TURNER: I don't want my children to have the time I had. I had a time, children, y'all don't know. Don't nobody know what a time I had. Oh, no.

[Mahalia Jackson singing "Hands on the Plow"]

JOHN CIARDI: You have to hear those best voices . . .

. . . says an American poet, as he recalls a childhood experience.

CIARDI: When I was a kid, my uncle used to have a tremendous collection of those scratchy old orthophonic Caruso recordings. And especially on rainy days, but all the time, I had a passion for Caruso. I heard him a couple of times live, but even on scratchy recordings—I remember him best on scratchy recordings . . .

[Caruso singing]

CIARDI: . . . because my memory of that is longest. But when you heard this voice, you not only heard the songs being sung; you suffered an expansion of your imagination. You discovered how well it was possible to sing these songs. Your very imagination was enlarged; you had a larger sense of expectation. You couldn't have anticipated these songs could have been sung so well. On two levels: in the first place you'd think just in the animal quality of the singing, Caruso would hit a high note and you'd think this is as much as the human voice can do; you couldn't ask more of the human voice. And then he'd be beyond that; he'd exceed the expectation. But there's another thing: it took centuries to form the kind of consciousness that would sing these songs in this way; the kind of musical intelligence that touched the songs perfectly at every moment. We're enlarged by it.

You have to hear those best voices. You have to open your imagination to Job asking his question, and when you have really heard that question *ringing*, you know the difference between a great question and a lesser one. Then you know the size of a human decision.

BERTRAND RUSSELL: As human beings, we have to remember that if the issues between the East and West are to be decided in any manner that can give any possible satisfaction to anybody—whether Communist or anti-Communist, whether Asian or European, or American, whether white or black—then these issues must not be decided by war. We should wish this to be understood, both in the East and in the West. There lies before us, if we choose, continual progress and happiness, knowledge and wisdom. Shall we instead choose death, because we cannot forget our quarrels? We appeal as human beings to human beings: Remember your humanity, and forget the rest. If you can do so, the way lies open to a new paradise. If you cannot, there lies before you the risk of universal death.

An eminent British philosopher poses the Great Question; and an American architect-designer recalls how that question came to be:

BUCKMINSTER FULLER: I said if Einstein is right, in due course, then, he is going to affect the other scientists, and the other scientists are going to affect all technology, and they're going to finally affect society. If that is so, why don't we look ahead? And part of this, earlier, when I spoke to you about a transcendental position, one of the things I said was let's go ahead and see what the world would be like if Einstein is right. . . . That year—let's see, we're talking about 1935—a few months later, Lise Meitner and her associate developed the first concept of fission—very shortly after that comes fission—and Einstein, then, when they were pretty sure that they had it, was asked to go to talk to Mr. Roosevelt about it, you may remember: the only man who could probably convince Mr. Roosevelt of its really important aspects. When fission was developed, then it proved Einstein's formula to be right: the amount of energy in the various masses proved to be exactly what his formula said. Therefore, the first practical application was a bomb to destroy man. I don't think it hit the people in Hiroshima as hard as it hit Mr. Einstein. I think he was really shocked. And he became, really, the scientist who alone really stood up; he, in his last days, did everything possible to try to make science think about its responsibilities. . . .

ALBERT EINSTEIN: We are gathered here at Princeton; this institution of research and scholarship represents a spiritual bond encompassing all countries. I am grateful to all for assisting us in our work. . . .

NICOLAI POGODIN [Speaking Russian; his interpreter translates]: We have a series published in the Soviet Union of books about great people, and I just happened to read the one about Einstein. . . . And after reading this book—it was like a novel to me; I read it day, night, day, night, until I finished it—and then I decided I have to write about this man. . . .

A Soviet playwright discusses the hero of his forthcoming drama.

POGODIN: But I want to say that the image of this great man has terribly impressed me as a human being. . . . This man has something in him which is so humane, so superb. The idea which is guiding me in this play is his tragedy; a tragedy in the Greek interpretation of this definition: he is guilty, but he is not guilty. The main idea by which I am guided and which is actually giving the tragedy its subjet is the following: that this great man came to us from the future into the present. It was tragically difficult for this man to live in this troubled world . . . divided and hostile world. I went to Princeton like a pilgrim goes to Mecca.

SEAN O'CASEY: It's an odd thing. Politics—I don't know why, but they seem to have a tendency to separate us, to keep us from one another, while Nature is always and ever making efforts to bring us closer together. The last gift that Nature has given us, a really extraordinary one, a very dangerous one, a very beautiful one, is the atom bomb. Nature, through the atom bomb, says, "Here you are: the power of darkness or the power of light. Choose what you wish." And mankind is going to choose the power of light!

ARTHUR C. CLARKE: I hope that we will make the wise choice, because everybody has agreed that the choice has to be made; and that extinction is the possibility of our generation— the first generation of mankind that's ever had this possibility in front of it . . .

A British writer of science fiction, in a moment of conjecture . . .

CLARKE: When you look out at the universe, there are a hundred thousand million suns in this galaxy of ours alone. And if only, say, one in ten has got planets, that may mean that to every single person on this earth, there's somewhere an inhabited world—that's about the number of inhabited worlds in this universe, one for every man, woman, and child on this earth—well, it seems very unlikely that on many of those there won't be races that would regard us as being somewhere back in the Stone Age.

Superior races, you said. You mean . . .

CLARKE: Well, I mean morally, intellectually, philosophically, technically . . .

No wars.

CLARKE: Well, a superior race cannot have war because war is a self-liquidating activity. . . . And I am optimistic about the outcome.

Either to destroy himself, or to be, perhaps, even more noble than ever, is that it?

CLARKE: Yes.

So the choice is ours.

CLARKE: The choice is ours. And it's really a privilege to be born in this age, the most critical in the whole history of mankind. I remember the old Chinese curse: "May you live in interesting times." Well, that curse has been visited on us, but I don't think it really is a curse. It's a privilege.

And it could be a blessing, too.

CLARKE: It could be.

HARLOW SHAPLEY: I've often wondered who would inherit the earth. We understand that the meek may inherit the earth; and, of course, that leaves us out. Will it be mammals, or will it be fish, or insects? . . .

A distinguished American astronomer on the subject of man, the elements, and risk . . .

SHAPLEY: In wondering about the future, and without actually trying to make a horoscope of humanity or of life on the earth, I have just tried to list down, sometimes, what are the risks we suffer. What will eliminate man, if he is eliminated from the surface of the earth? Will it be the sun running down, or blowing up; either one of those? Freezing man out or incinerating him? No, because the sun's a good steady star, and as you know it's pretty well thermostated to run for, say, ten thousand million years at its present rate. So the sun isn't going to play out. How about stars colliding with us? No, they're too far apart. Collisions happen too infrequently. Say, in the next thousand centuries: no, no chance of that. I mean a very low chance. Well, what about the earth getting out of its orbit and running away and freezing to death in empty space? Or plunging into the sun and boiling up? No chance. We know from our celestial mechanics that the orbit of the earth is constant, and will stay just about put. And so, I think we're safe from sun, from star, from earth. So now, must I say that it looks pretty safe for man for this future you talk about for the next thousand centuries? Yes? No! Because he has one deadly enemy that I didn't mention; an enemy that's at his throat and may succeed in returning him to the fossils and leaving life on the earth to the cockroaches and the kelp. You know what that enemy is, of course? That's man himself.

[Myoka Harubasa's despairing voice, then the Weavers singing]

Will there be time to find salvation
Will there be time to find salvation
Will there be time to find salvation,
When the stars begin to fall?

[Gradually a cello builds beneath the following words]

ALEXANDER ELIOT: This picture of the two men clobbering each other in the quicksand in the valley, at the Prado, is first of all a horrible picture; a shocking picture. After that you begin to see it within the context of this magnificent landscape: all a silver, somber, magnificently harmonious thing . . . and in the midst of it are these two bloody idiots. And you see that if you could only get through to them somehow, and tell them what they're doing, and how they are denying by their very action the beauty and the harmony and the mystery that surrounds them—they're denying the fact that they're equally children of God, equally brothers—somehow they would recognize what Goya so poignantly makes you realize in looking at the picture.

LILLIAN SMITH: "Who am I?" "Where am I going?" "What is death?" "Who is God?" "Why am I here?" . . . Here now we all ask; children ask, and the Greeks ask, and existential philosophers ask, and every thoughtful person: "Who am I?"

[The Weavers sing]

My Lord, What a morning
My Lord, What a morning
My Lord, What a morning
When the stars begin to fall.

A British scientist writes of a particular moment in his life:

"On a fine November day in 1945, late in the afternoon, I was landed on an airstrip in southern Japan. I did not know that we had left the open country until, unexpectedly, I heard the ship's loudspeakers broadcasting dance music."

[We hear strains of "Is You Is, or Is You Ain't My Baby?"]

"Then, suddenly, I was aware that we were already at the center of damage in Nagasaki. The shadows behind me were the skeleton of the Mitsubishi factory building, pushed backwards and sidewise as if by a giant hand. What I had thought to be broken rocks was a concrete powerhouse with its roof punched in. I could make out nothing but cockeyed telegraph poles, and loops of wire in a bare waste of ashes. I had blundered into this desolate landscape as instantly as one might wake among the mountains of the moon. The moment of recognition when I realized that I was already in Nagasaki is present to me as I write as vividly as when I lived it. I see the warm night and the meaningless shapes. I can even remember the tune that was coming from the ship."

[We hear the lyrics: "Yes, I'm gonna ask him: Is you is, or is you ain't my baby?"]

"This dissertation was born at that moment. For the moment I recall was a universal moment. What I met was almost as abruptly the experience of mankind. On an evening sometime in 1945, each of us in his own way learned that his imagination had been dwarfed. We looked up and saw the power of which we had been proud loom over us like the ruins of Nagasaki. The power of science for good and for evil has troubled other minds than ours. We are not here fumbling with a new dilemma; our subject and our fears are as old as the tool-making civilizations. Nothing happened except that we changed the scale of our indifference to man. And conscience for an instant became immediate to us. Let us acknowledge our subject for what it is: civilization, face-to-face with its own implications. The implications are both the industrial slum which Nagasaki was before it was bombed, and the ashy desolation which the bomb made of the slum. And civilization asks of both ruins: [Pause] Is you is, or is you ain't my baby?"

REV. WILLIAM SLOANE COFFIN JR.: Let us pray. [Pause] Lord, number us, we beseech thee, in the ranks of those who went forth from this university longing only for those things for which thou dost make us long; men for whom the complexity of issues only serve to renew their zeal to deal with them; men who alleviated pain by sharing it; and the men who were always willing to risk something big for something good. So may we leave in the world a little more truth, a little more justice, a little more beauty than would have been there had we not loved the world enough to quarrel with it for what it is not, but still could be. Oh, God, take our minds and think through them; take our lips and speak through them; and take our hearts and set them on fire. Amen.

GEORGIA TURNER: Sometime I look up . . . I don't have to do nothin' . . . just stand and look up there . . . and look up towards the Father. When I look up towards the Father, the tears come rollin' down and tie a bouquet under my neck. I say, "Lord, here I am." When the storm and the wind get to tossin' the tent from side to side, I call up the Boss and tell Him. I say, "Lord, here I am. I ain't even got a shelter; I ain't even got a frame around me. I say, "You know me. Remember me, here. Take care." Because I'm striving to make Heaven my home. I'm working to make Heaven my home. I'm bearin' my burden. I'm bearin' down in the morning, yes, I'm cryin' in the evening sometimes, you know, tryin' to make Heaven my home. That's what it takes. I got to love everybody. I can't hate nobody . . .

[Strains of "I'm on My Way" playing]

TURNER: If you do me wrong, I still don't hate you for it. No. Because I'm on my way. And I don't see nothin' to turn me back. I'm on my way!

[Mahalia Jackson singing "I'm on My Way, to Canaan Land"]

CARL SANDBURG: Man is a long time coming.
Man will yet win.
Brother the earth over may yet line up with brother:
This old anvil, the people, yes.

This old anvil, that laughs at many broken hammers.

There are men who can't be bought.

There are women beyond purchase.

The fire-born are at home in fire.

The stars make no noise.

You can't hinder the wind from blowing.

Time is a great teacher.

Who can live without hope?

In the darkness with a great bundle of grief the people march.

In the night, and overhead a shovel of stars for keeps, the people march:

"Where to? What next?"

Where to? What next?

[There is a slight pause; then we hear Eric Naess, the baby, just learning to talk, say "Hoppy! Hoppy! Hoppy!"]

[Pete Seeger strums the fourth movement of Beethoven's Ninth Symphony on his banjo as Studs Terkel reads the closing credits.]

For thirty-one years, we played Born to Live *on our radio station at 11 a.m. every New Year's morning. At 11:05, as reliably as Big Ben, the phone rang. It was the baby, Eric, who mumbled in broken English, "Happy, happy, happy." Every year, the broadcast, followed by that call. Through the years, I discovered he sang in a children's choral group. As he aged, his voice deepened to a bass baritone. I learned Eric became a ranger because he loved the woodlands. When last I heard from him he had become a labor organizer.*

ACKNOWLEDGMENTS

My salute to Sydney Lewis, my right hand; JR Millares, my caregiver and companion; and my son Dan, everlastingly on the watch. I bow deeply to Connie Hall for her remarkable detective work in tracking down the date and circumstances of the Chicago monthly journal vignettes, and offer my thanks to Lois Baum for coming through with several pertinent suggestions. A doff of my cap to the New Press staff, especially Jyothi Natarajan and Maury Botton, and gratitude always to my longtime publisher, André Schiffrin.

SOURCES

"Scaring the Daylights Out of Ma Perkins, 1974" first appeared in the *Chicago Guide* 23:2 (February 1974), 110–113, 192.

"Dreamland, 1977" first appeared in *Chicago* 26:4 (April 1977), 127–129.

"City of Hands Was Born in Mud and Fire" first appeared in *Financial Times,* September 10, 2005. Reprinted with permission of *Financial Times.*

"Vince Garrity, 1974" first appeared in the *Chicago Guide* 23:8 (August 1974), 88–89, 99.

"Frank Tuller, in Memoriam, 1975" first appeared in *Chicago* 24:7 (July 1975), 86–87.

"Who's Got the Ballot?—Red Kelly, 1975" first appeared in *Chicago* 24:1 (January 1975), 64–67.

"Ya Gotta Fight City Hall, 1973" first appeared in the *Chicago Guide* 22:9 (September 1973), 145–147.

"Nighthawks, 1971" first appeared in a *Life* magazine book review by Studs Terkel.

"A Christmas Memory, 1973" first appeared in the *Chicago Guide* 22:12 (December 1973), 128–131.

"Suffer the Little Children, 1980" first appeared in *Chicago,* February 1980.

"A Family Bar, 1979" first appeared in *Chicago,* January 1979.

"Aaron Barkham" first appeared in *Hard Times* (New York: The New Press, 2000), 202–206. Reprinted with permission of The New Press.

"A Voice from a 'Hey, You' Neighborhood, 1973" first appeared in the *Chicago Guide* 22:11 (November 1973), 150–151.